Discovering MS™-DOS

* fff*

HOWARD W. SAMS & COMPANY/HAYDEN BOOKS

Related Titles

MS-DOS® Developer's Guide
John Angermeyer and Kevin Jaeger, The Waite Group

MS-DOS® Bible
Steven Simrin, The Waite Group

Discovering MS-DOS®
Kate O'Day, The Waite Group

C Programmer's Guide to Serial Communications
Joe Campbell

Microsoft® C Programming on the IBM®
Robert Lafore, The Waite Group

Inside XENIX®
Christopher L. Morgan, The Waite Group

C Primer Plus, Revised Edition
Mitchell Waite, Stephen Prata, and Donald Martin, The Waite Group

Advanced C Primer ++
Stephen Prata, The Waite Group

C with Excellence
Henry F. Ledgard

*For the retailer nearest you, or to order directly from the publisher,
call 800-428-SAMS. In Indiana, Alaska, and Hawaii call 317-298-5699.*

Discovering MS-DOS

Kate O'Day

HOWARD W. SAMS & COMPANY

A Division of Macmillan, Inc.
4300 West 62nd Street
Indianapolis, Indiana 46268 USA

FIRST EDITION
FIFTH PRINTING — 1988

International Standard Book Number: 0-672-22407-0
Library of Congress Catalog Card Number: 84-52513

Edited by *Susan Pink Bussiere* and *Douglas P. DeBrabant*
Illustrated by *T. R. Emrick*
Cartoons by *Bob Johnson*
Printed in the United States of America

Preface

MS-DOS is the powerful disk operating system developed by Microsoft for use in today's microcomputers. It provides the instructions that enable microcomputers to manipulate files, handle interactions between the computer and the user, and manage peripherals.

Today's typical computer user is not interested in programming. With the wealth of application programs on the market today, users can survive nicely without ever learning much about the software "heart" of their systems. But by learning how to make use of the power of MS-DOS, you can increase the ease with which you use your system. Certain procedures can be streamlined, information can be stored and accessed rapidly, and MS-DOS shortcuts can make using a computer easier than ever.

In *Discovering MS-DOS,* you will embark on an exciting and educational voyage of discovery to the most popular disk operating system for microcomputers today. MS-DOS provides your computer with the instructions that make it perform its amazing feats, from running a spreadsheet program and filing letters to playing games and watching the stock market. While most users barely scratch the surface when using their systems, *Discovering MS-DOS* will show you how to master this powerful software tool, thus expanding the usefulness of your system in a way that is both informative and fun.

This book is different from many books on MS-DOS and other operating systems in several ways. First, you don't need a computer background to read it. Second, it is written with the belief that computer concepts don't have to be complicated or boring. They can be presented in an entertaining way and still be instructive. Third, when you have finished this book, you will find that in addition to having fun reading it and working the examples, you will have learned how to utilize the power of MS-DOS.

Discovering MS-DOS begins with a description of what a computer is and why it needs an operating system. You then learn how to start your system, how to handle diskettes, and how to get information into and out of your system. You are shown how to maximize the editing capabilities of MS-DOS's line editor, EDLIN, and how to shape up your files. Then you move into high gear and learn about the power of the keyboard—function keys and keystroke combinations that can make everyday tasks easier. Ways to develop routines so that repetitive tasks are automated are shown in a clear and entertaining style. The real power of MS-DOS is revealed in the tree-structured directories and pathnames of version 2.0 (and above), and the advanced features of redirection, piping, and filtering. For the hard disk user, the BACKUP and RESTORE commands are explained clearly and concisely. An appendix explains the most common error messages in MS-DOS, and possible solutions. A reference card is included to provide a handy summary of MS-DOS commands.

The author has used MS-DOS on a variety of microcomputers, and has been involoved in the development of training programs and user orientation. This background has helped her identify the areas where users, new to the world of computers and MS-DOS in particular, have the most difficulty; and it has allowed her to guide you in your journey of discovery without tripping. The author hopes that you not only learn about this important part of your microcomputer system, but that you enjoy yourself along the way.

KATE O'DAY

Dedication

To Seamus Matthew Mercer Hursh—who, waiting patiently for his trip to the beach or to see the latest movie, has no choice but to be part of the "computer generation." This book's for you!

Acknowledgments

I would like to thank Kim House for starting me off on the right path and helping develop the concept for *Discovering MS-DOS*. My special thanks to Mary Johnson not only for her sensitive editing but also for her patience and understanding throughout the course of writing this book. Finally, my thanks to Bob Johnson for his cartoons which help illustrate that learning computer concepts can be entertaining.

CONTENTS

Introduction

Let Me Introduce You to MS-DOS

- Welcome MS-DOS Users
- What You Need to Use This Book
- What's in *Discovering MS-DOS*

Introduction
Let Me Introduce You to MS-DOS

Welcome MS-DOS Users

This book is about using your computer system. It is especially for new computer owners. To read, use, and enjoy *Discovering MS-DOS* you don't have to know a thing about MS-DOS, operating systems, or even computer terminology. The only thing you need to know right now is that MS-DOS is the operating system that comes with your computer.

You may have some doubts that you really know what a computer system *is*. You may be a little unclear on what a computer system *does*. And you're all but sure that you don't know how to *operate* a computer system. Relax, you've come to the right place. Together we're going to explore MS-DOS and this guided tour will stop at all points of major interest. At the end of this journey you're going to be a confident and experienced MS-DOS user.

This book is particularly about *MS-DOS,* one of the most popular operating systems used in microcomputers today. It is available for a wide variety of computers ranging from self-contained portables to the many IBM PC compatibles. The IBM PC itself uses a special version of MS-DOS. While there may be slight differences in the way that MS-DOS is implemented, this book will help you discover the power of this operating system.

Discovering MS-DOS employs a well-known educational technique— "Learning by doing." Computer folks have translated this into the "hands-on approach." Whichever term you prefer, this book is not only descriptive, it presents examples and exercises for each part of MS-DOS. You will get your "hands wet" typing information into the computer and seeing the results of your labor. These projects are designed to help you *really* understand the information being discussed.

What You Need to Use This Book

To use this book you need a personal computer equipped with a keyboard, monitor, and the MS-DOS operating system. You also need at least one disk drive (two are preferable). Much of the material presented is applicable to MS-DOS Versions 1.0 and 1.1. However, *Discovering MS-DOS* is aimed principally at users of MS-DOS Version 2.0 or higher. If you have MS-DOS Version 3.0, this book provides information on fundamentals that you need to make full use of your system.

If you have the above equipment, an MS DOS diskette, and a willing mind, you're ready to begin this adventure.

What's in *Discovering MS-DOS*

If this is your first experience with computers, the layout of this book is for you. You just start with Chapter 1, "This Is a Computer System," and don't look back. In Chapter 1, you will get an introduction to computer systems. Then in Chapter 2, "This Is an Operating System," you will gain some knowledge about operating systems in general. You will begin using your operating system in Chapter 3, "Getting MS-DOS off the Ground." If you are already familiar with the components of a computer system, and understand what an operating system is and does, you can go directly to Chapter 3.

Chapter 4, "System Insurance," shows you how to protect your investment in MS-DOS by explaining how to care for and make copies of your diskettes. Chapter 5, "Minding Your E's and Q's," lets your creativity shine through by explaining the operation of the EDLIN line editing program that comes with MS-DOS. With this program you can write letters, memos, and other long documents and make changes and corrections as you go along. All of the EDLIN commands are explained here for you. Chapter 6, "Getting the Files in Shape," really expands your understanding of MS-DOS by leading you step-by-step through file creation, naming, and command use. You will learn how to look at a file, to copy a file, to rename files, and how to erase files. In Chapter 7, "Shifting into High Gear," the real power of the keyboard and the function keys is described. You will learn techniques to speed up entering and changing data, as well as how certain key combinations can enhance your use of your system. Chapter 8, "Mixing up a Fresh Batch," will make your routine use of MS-DOS even handier. You

will learn what batch files are and how they can make your job easier. You will see how to program your system to perform many functions automatically.

After learning all the interesting things that your MS-DOS equipped system can do for you, Chapter 9, "You Can See the Forest for the Trees," will show you how to organize your information files into easy-to-use directories, as well as show you how to rapidly access the data that you have so carefully arranged. For those of you without hard disk drive systems, Chapter 10, "Plumbing Techniques," will bring you to the end of your studies. You will learn how to make your system direct, sort, and find data and files in such a way that you will wonder why you waited so long to acquire your computer. Chapter 11, "For Hard Disk Users," will be of interest to non-hard disk users as well because it explains the advantages and disadvantages of both types of systems (floppy or hard disk). It also shows the hard disk user how to perform two very critical hard disk operations, backing up and restoring information on the disk system. By moving through the chapters, you will find that you will gradually build on your growing knowledge of MS-DOS. The chapters are best read in order. Of course, once you have finished this book it will be a valuable reference tool. For quick, concise reference we have included a pull-out DOS Reference Card at the end.

So fasten your seat belts, and let's begin!

HOWARD W. SAMS & COMPANY

DEAR VALUED CUSTOMER:

Howard W. Sams & Company is dedicated to bringing you timely and authoritative books for your personal and professional library. Our goal is to provide you with excellent technical books written by the most qualified authors. You can assist us in this endeavor by checking the box next to your particular areas of interest.

We appreciate your comments and will use the information to provide you with a more comprehensive selection of titles.

Thank you,

Vice President, Book Publishing
Howard W. Sams & Company

COMPUTER TITLES:

Hardware
- ☐ Apple 140   ☐ Macintosh I01
- ☐ Commodore I10
- ☐ IBM & Compatibles I14

Business Applications
- ☐ Word Processing J01
- ☐ DataBase J04
- ☐ Spreadsheets J02

Operating Systems
- ☐ MS-DOS K05   ☐ OS/2 K10
- ☐ CP/M K01   ☐ UNIX K03

Programming Languages
- ☐ C L03   ☐ Pascal L05
- ☐ Prolog L12   ☐ Assembly L01
- ☐ BASIC L02   ☐ HyperTalk L14

Troubleshooting & Repair
- ☐ Computers S05
- ☐ Peripherals S10

Other
- ☐ Communications/Networking M03
- ☐ AI/Expert Systems T18

ELECTRONIC TITLES:
- ☐ Amateur Radio T01
- ☐ Audio T03
- ☐ Basic Electronics T20
- ☐ Basic Electricity T21
- ☐ Electronic Design T12
- ☐ Electronic Projects T04
- ☐ Satellites T09

- ☐ Instrumentation T05
- ☐ Digital Electronics T11

Troubleshooting & Repair
- ☐ Audio S11   ☐ Television S04
- ☐ VCR S01   ☐ Compact Disc S02
- ☐ Automotive S06
- ☐ Microwave Oven S03

Other interests or comments: _____

_____

_____

Name_____

Title _____

Company _____

Address _____

City _____

State/Zip _____

Daytime Telephone No. _____

A Division of Macmillan, Inc.

4300 West 62nd Street   Indianapolis, Indiana 46268

22407

Book Mark

fff

HOWARD W. SAMS
& COMPANY

Book Mark

HOWARD W. SAMS & COMPANY

1

This Is a Computer System

- What Is a Computer System?
- Hardware
  - Central Processing Unit (Microprocessor)
  - Memory
  - Storage Devices
- Software
  - Application Programs
  - Programming Languages
  - Operating Systems

1   This Is a Computer System

What Is a Computer System?

A microcomputer system can range from a small "portable" machine that you can store under an airplane seat, to a desktop machine with fancy graphics capabilities and three printers. Most likely, your machine falls somewhere in between. MS-DOS is available for most all of these machines and many more that fall inside the broad definition of "computer system."

This book will help make your learning experience more enjoyable. But you may sometimes be confused when our discussion or illustrations do not match your specific computer layout. Since MS-DOS is available for many types of computers, our discussion will deal with general definitions and components of computer systems, and generic elements of MS-DOS. If at times you are confused about specific names, displays, keys, or messages, check the manual that the manufacturer packages with your system.

In this chapter, we are going to take a look at the parts of your computer system, both inside and out. This discussion is just to get you started on the road to building a "computer vocabulary." These are "terms" that help make operating MS-DOS easier. Don't worry about *knowing* these words, no memorization is necessary.

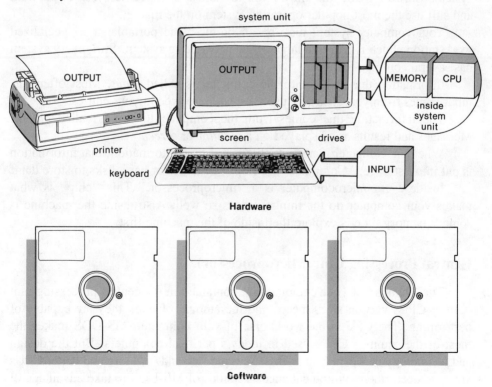

Hardware and software.

Your computer system is made up of many different components. The machine parts are called *hardware*. This includes your keyboard, disk drives, and monitor. You can connect *peripherals* (additional hardware) to your machine through specialized *ports* or *connectors* (the places where they "plug into" your machine). One typical peripheral is a printer.

The part of your computer system that makes this hardware perform is called *software*—the programs that control the operation of your machine. You are already acquainted somewhat with one type of software, your MS-DOS operating system. Other types of software include application programs (e.g., word-processors, games, accounting packages) and utility programs (e.g., sorting programs and printing routines). Software also includes programming languages such as BASIC, and assembly language programs that communicate directly with your computer in the machine's native language.

Hardware

One of the advantages of MS-DOS is the ability of many machines to operate with this system. This simply means that MS-DOS is the operating system that "controls" how the computer performs its work. Since many types of computer systems run MS-DOS, this allows you to choose the specific system you want and still use the most popular operating system on the market.

Your computer system may be an on-the-plane portable or a specialized workstation which is part of a large office networking system. Still, every system has several common features.

Information that is fed into the computer is called *input*. Most often this input comes from you. You will use a *keyboard* to type in your entries.

The information that comes from the computer to you is called *output*. Messages and results are displayed on a *monitor* or *screen*.

When the computer is not actually using some information, that information is put into "storage." Computers use floppy diskettes or hard disks to store data.

Inside every microcomputer is a "microprocessor." This "chip" is what makes your computer do the things it does so well. Also inside the machine is some "memory." Let's explore the inside of the machine first.

Central Processing Unit (Microprocessor)

The "brains" of your computer are contained in the central processing unit (CPU). CPUs vary in size, speed, and the amount of work they are capable of performing. The CPU is the workhorse of your computer. MS-DOS makes the most of the common CPUs used in today's personal computers. But the design and technology of CPUs is growing at a rapid rate and, as more and better CPUs are developed, there will be enhanced versions of MS-DOS to take advantage of the latest advances in technology.

Memory

The computer has two types of memory, each with very specific characteristics.

Random Access Memory (RAM) is memory which is used by the computer to hold the information it is currently working on. Information in RAM changes as you edit and enter data. It is very important to remember that RAM is *transient*. Things stored in RAM are only temporary, when you turn off the machine, RAM is wiped clean.

You must transfer any data or programs in RAM to storage (on a diskette or hard disk) before you turn off your machine. Application programs, which come

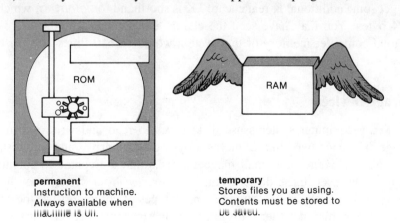

permanent
Instruction to machine.
Always available when
machine is on.

temporary
Stores files you are using.
Contents must be stored to
be saved.

ROM and RAM.

on their own diskettes, or information that you do not alter and already have on a diskette do not need to be returned to storage at the end of a working session.

Read Only Memory (ROM), on the other hand, is permanent. It is actually contained in hardware on your CPU. ROM contents are determined by your computer manufacturer.

The amount of memory in your computer is measured in *bytes*. Each byte contains eight *bits*. A byte can be thought of as one character. As I enter this text on my word processor, it takes six bytes to store "MS-DOS" (actually eight, if you count the quotation marks).

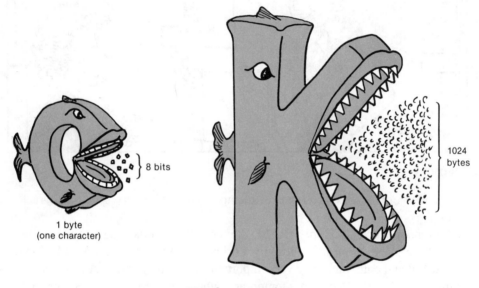

8 bits

1 byte
(one character)

1024
bytes

Bits, bytes, and K.

Computer memory is often described in terms of *K*, as in "I know where I can get some additional K real cheap!" K is shorthand for *kilobytes*, which means 1024 bytes. You may have seen the claim "expandable to 640K." This means the total computer memory of that system would be 640 times 1024 or 655,360 bytes.

Storage Devices

Many computer systems use disk drives to read and write information to storage. There are two kinds of drives, floppy diskette drives and hard disk drives.

Floppy diskettes are small magnetic disks that are coated to contain information. You insert these diskettes into *disk drives*. Your system may have one, two, or several disk drives. Although many types of computers use the same size diskettes, you may not (generally) interchange diskettes between different types of machines. This is because computers place information on diskettes in various ways.

Hard disk drives can be built into your machine or they can be external "peripherals." The hard disk inside one of these drives is not removable. The advantages of hard disks are that they can store much more information than floppy disks and they are faster than floppies. However, they are also more expensive.

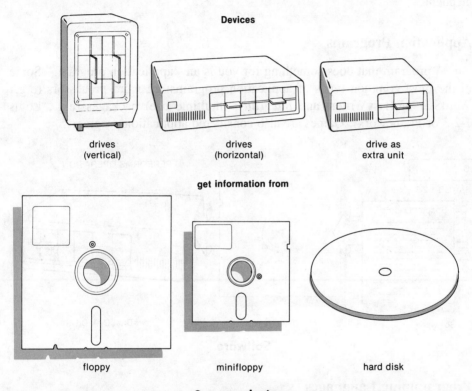

Devices

drives (vertical) drives (horizontal) drive as extra unit

get information from

floppy minifloppy hard disk

Storage devices.

As mentioned earlier, disks store programs and data that you are not actively using. Information is read from the disk into the computer's RAM (temporary) memory. As you need more information, the drive retrieves it from your diskette. When you are finished working, the information is sent to the diskette for storage.

These are the basic terms associated with hardware that will help you understand using MS-DOS.

If you understand a few terms that apply to software, that may clear up some confusion you may be experiencing whenever you venture inside your friendly computer store. A quick definition of these will boost your computer confidence considerably.

Software

According to buying experts, when choosing a computer system you should first find the software you want and then buy the computer to fit the software's specifications. That's how important the software is in a computer system. While you want convenience and ease of use in the system hardware, if the software does not do what you want, you really have nothing but an easy-to-use white elephant.

Application Programs

A program that does something for you is an "application program." Some of the most common types of application programs are word processors (e.g., WordStar or EasyWriter) and *integrated* (multiple use) packages (e.g., Lotus 1-2-3 or Framework). Games are also considered application programs.

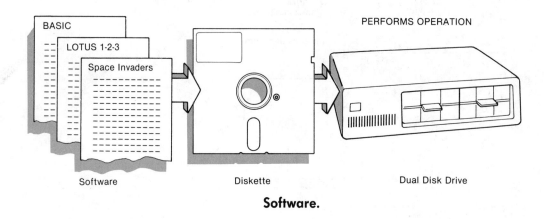

BASIC		PERFORMS OPERATION
LOTUS 1-2-3		
Space Invaders		

Software   Diskette   Dual Disk Drive

Software.

Programming Languages

Another type of software lets you write instructions, in the form of programs, for your computer. This software is known as a programming language. You use these languages to design your own "application" programs. Your computer probably uses the BASIC programming language. BASIC may be contained inside ROM memory, or you may have it on your operating system diskette. Other programming languages include Pascal, Logo, and Cobol.

Operating Systems

Yes, your operating system is a type of specialized software. The operating system manages all the disk input and output operations of your computer. You are an important part of the input and output system since you are the originator and receiver of this input and output. How well you, the information, and the machine all work together is the secret of an effective operating system. In Chapter 2 you will learn about the "secret life of MS-DOS."

This first chapter has served several purposes. For those of you unfamiliar with computers, it defined some useful computer terms: hardware, software, memory, storage, and input and output. Along the way it introduced most of the parts of your computer system that are used in the operation of MS-DOS.

This Is an Operating System

- What Does an Operating System Do?
- How Did Operating Systems Evolve?
- History of MS-DOS
- What MS-DOS Means to You

2   This Is an Operating System

This chapter explains what an operating system is, what it does for the computer, and what it can do for you. It also takes a brief look at the evolution of operating systems, the history of MS-DOS, and the unique position of MS-DOS in the operating system world of today.

When you first encountered the term *operating system,* it was probably in the small print of an advertisement or part of an eager salesperson's technobabble. Among all those other incomprehensible terms, such as RAM, ROM, modem, expandability, peripherals, RS232, and CPU, its significance may have escaped you. Computer advertising may seem at times to be based on several thoughts: that a lot of information is better than a little, double talk or jargon is a virtue, and the longer and more obscure the word, the better.

But *operating system* is not a complex or confusing concept. Let's start with definitions from the *Random House Dictionary of the English Language:*

Operate 1. to work or perform a function, like a machine does. 2. to work or use a machine.

Well, that's pretty clear, operate has to do with performing machine-like actions.

System 1. A complex or unitary whole. 2. A coordinated body of methods or a complex scheme or plan of procedure.

So, an operating system is a coordinated body of methods or a plan of procedure for controlling machines. MS-DOS, the operating system in your computer, organizes the information that goes into and comes out of the machine and it controls how the parts of your computer system interact. The operating system runs the computer.

What Does an Operating System Do?

As you read in Chapter 1, a computer system is a collection of *hardware,* the machine parts, and *software,* the instructions that tell the computer how to perform the actual computing operations.

You use the hardware, such as the keyboard, disk drives, monitor, and printer, to coordinate data. Hardware provides the tools to type in data, feed data to or from a diskette, receive data from other machines, or copy it to the printer.

Software, usually in the form of *programs,* gives instructions to the computer. Software tells the computer what to do, at what time, and with what data. Without software, the hardware is as useless as the abandoned shell of a 1965 Mustang convertible. It's beautiful but powerless.

The main function of the operating system is to manage the information you enter into, store in, and retrieve from your computer.

In the course of its work, the operating system acts as an interface between you, who understand what you would like to happen to the data you type in, and the mechanics of the computer, which demand that instructions be in a form that can be "understood." Let's see how MS-DOS responds to this challenge.

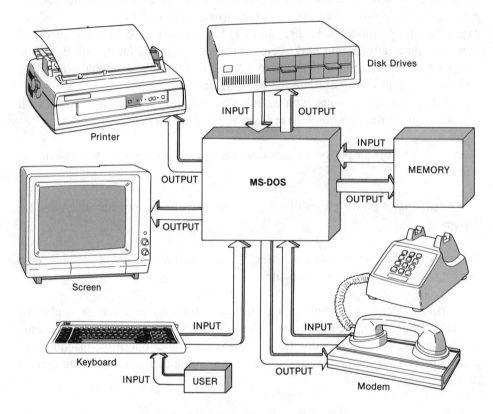

Managing files is DOS's main job!

The major responsibility of the operating system is to keep all the incoming and outgoing information in order. MS-DOS accomplishes this task by storing information in *files*. Computer files are no different from paper files, both hold a collection of related data. You give each file a name and the operating system does the rest, storing the file where it can find it quickly, updating the file when you enter new information, and even eliminating the file when you don't want it anymore. Computers may not be terribly interesting to converse with, but they are very good file clerks.

If this idea of a master program still seems a bit obscure, let's compare it to something equally complex in everyday life. Suppose that instead of speaking of a DOS ("DOS" is an acronym for *disk operating system*), we were speaking of an ATC (air traffic controller). This ATC is in charge of all operations at a major international airport.

The controller is responsible for coordinating the overall traffic flow. He is constantly aware of which planes are coming in, on which runways they'll land, their speed, and their arrival gates. He must be sure those runways and gates have been cleared for landing. He must know the relative position of each plane waiting to take off and which flight paths they will follow as they ascend. And he must often make quick decisions so that all planes arrive and depart on schedule.

Listening to the conversation in a control tower is like landing on another planet. You know that the instructions being passed back and forth are in English, but it's hard to believe these people are conversing sensibly. It might sound something like this:

"United 9er9er 7 heavy, clear for take-off on 2-1-left. You're number 3 behind the company."

You can't really understand it, but obviously it's working.

Well, the operating system is like that controller. It monitors all the incoming and outgoing activity of your computer system. Just as the controller is in constant contact with the position of every plane in the air or on the ground, the operating system knows the location and size of all the files currently in its memory or stored on its current disk. And like the controller, the operating system constantly updates all of its information according to changing conditions.

The controller's job is to make sure that each plane scheduled to come into the airport does indeed arrive and each plane scheduled to leave does disappear into the wild blue yonder. Again, the operating system does much the same thing for your computer programs and data files. It loads them, makes sure they start executing, and when one is finished, it makes room for the next.

This kind of organizational control sounds like a pretty handy helper to have, whether you are navigating the skies over Chicago, or attempting to get your accounting software to run. But just as the Wright Brothers had to struggle along on their own, so too did early computer operators. Operating systems are a fairly recent innovation in computer operation. Let's see how operating systems came to be.

How Did Operating Systems Evolve?

The earliest commercially available computers were physically large, yet simple-minded, machines. You put your instructions on punch cards (all the cards in one group usually made up a *program*) and handed them to the computer "operator." When it was time for your program to run, the first instruction told the computer to come "on." After the operator fiddled with some switches or

controls, the computer started, read your instructions, executed your program, and then stopped (although often it just skipped the middle two steps and stopped). The operator would then clear the machine and prepare for the next program. Early computers could only run one program at a time. To them, only the program in the computer at that time existed. As a consequence, the computer spent a great deal of time sitting idle.

Many people in the still small, yet quickly growing, computer industry sensed the waste of all this "down time." They began to see the advantage of some type of standardized start-up procedure for the computer. If the instructions to run each program were the same, then several programs could be run in quick succession. What they needed was to take out the human's job and make the computer run itself. This was the birth of the "operating system" concept.

According to popular reports, the first mention of a computer operating system took place at the 1953 Eastern Joint Computer Conference. Sitting around in a hotel room, some IBM programmers came up with the concept of a *monitor program*. It was the first development of a program designed simply to "run the machine." The monitor program kept track of a number of "jobs," or programs. When a job was completed, control returned to the monitor program which then started up the next job.

Operating systems (expanded monitor programs) for mainframe computers became a reality. But the standardization was limited to each machine. This was fine for a while because there weren't very many computers and the programs you wrote were designed to run on one specific type. But these early computer pioneers could hardly forsee the rapid growth of computers. Shrinking in size, while gaining in power and ease of use, computers quickly became a vital part of business and government. With this growth came the need for more standardized programs. No longer could a program be designed for a machine, not when the market was there to sell many copies to other users.

And then, in 1975, it happened. The first real "home computer," named the ALTAIR, appeared on the cover of *Popular Electronics*. Manufactured by a company called MITS, this computer kit, designed for hobbyists, retailed for $397.00 and could be built (with sufficient technical knowledge) in your garage. Computing had come to the masses. Visionaries began to see a time when computers would be in every classroom, even in every home. These computers would need to be easy to use. They would need to run many kinds of programs. They would need a standardized way to handle the information stored in their files. They would need, in short, a common operating system.

History of MS-DOS

One of those who was impressed by the possibilities of the ALTAIR computer was William Gates. In 1975, Gates was studying at Harvard. No computer novice even then, Gates and his friend Paul Allen had been working with computers since they were in seventh grade. But the introduction of the new, small ALTAIR really stirred their imaginations. They knew these "hobbyist computers" would need a simple, reliable programming language. No problem, they would adapt the widely used BASIC language to this new type of smaller machine. After convincing MITS that "their" BASIC was up and running, Gates and Allen spent four frantic weeks writing a simulated program on an available mainframe computer. Incredibly, the language they devised worked on its first try! Today that BASIC is the standard programming language on millions of personal computers.

The success of their BASIC sent Gates and Allen into the computer business in earnest. Always aware of the escalating importance of standardization, they developed and sold several adaptations of programming languages. The company they formed was called Microsoft.

In July of 1981, Microsoft purchased the rights to 86-DOS, an operating system developed by Seattle Computer Products. In secret they began working with IBM, developing this system to be used as the PC-DOS operating system for IBM's personal computer (the IBM PC).

Microsoft released its version of the operating system (MS-DOS) to the general public in March of 1982. In February 1983, an enhanced version of MS-DOS, version 2.0, appeared. This is probably the version of MS-DOS that you have on your computer.

What MS-DOS Means to You

Every computer needs an operating system. But the fact that your computer uses the MS-DOS operating system brings you some extra advantages.

Since the operating system is the interface between you and your computer's operation, you want it to be easy to use. MS-DOS more than fills this bill. It is relatively clearly written and simple to learn. Most of the operations you want to accomplish can be performed with a few, easy-to-understand commands. Yet MS-DOS also incorporates some very sophisticated and complex functions in its structure. As your computer knowledge grows, so will your appreciation of MS-DOS's capabilities.

One of the the biggest advantages of MS-DOS is its popularity. Because MS-DOS is the chosen operating system of so many personal computer manufacturers, software programmers have responded with a deluge of application programs. This means you can usually find the programs you want right away and they will work with no modifications on your machine.

This chapter discussed the concept of an operating system. It told you that MS-DOS manages files to keep track of the information put into the computer. It also discussed the development of operating systems from their first use on mainframe computers to their use on the personal computers of today. Finally, it traced the growth of MS-DOS from a vision in the eyes of Gates and Allen to its current popularity in the operating systems market.

3

Getting MS-DOS
off the Ground

3   Getting MS-DOS off the Ground

Now that you are familiar with the basic facts about computer systems and you know that MS-DOS helps operate your system, it's time to put two and two together and begin computing. You probably agree that this sounds like a good plan, but you may have no idea about how to begin. Well, just as a pilot approaches take off in a logical step-by-step fashion, so you are going to follow a simple routine for your "pre-flight checklist."

First, make sure that your machine is properly set up and ready to go (your user's manual will give you all the necessary instructions). Second, sit down at the controls. Just as the cockpit of an airplane may seem intimidating to you, so may the intricacies of actually being in command of your computer.

But using MS-DOS is very simple. In this chapter you will learn how to "boot" your system, how to activate the built-in calendar and clock, and how to get the computer to respond to MS-DOS commands. Two commands are introduced in this chapter, the DIR (directory) command and the CLS (clear the screen) command. (The CLS command isn't available on MS-DOS Versions 1.0 and 1.1.) So put on your captain's hat and let's get off the ground.

First Things First

To begin using your computer, you must "boot" the system. This does not mean you deliver a sharp kick to the backside of the machine! The term is derived from "pulling oneself up by the bootstraps." In computereze, boot means getting the machine ready to accept your instructions.

This sounds very simple, but logically it creates a Catch-22 problem. How can the machine start, if the instructions it needs to begin are located inside the machine (which you can't get to until the machine starts)?

This problem is solved by a handy little program called, you guessed it, the "bootstrap loader." This small program, located in ROM (that's the part of memory that is permanent), is the first thing the computer reads when the power is turned on. The bootstrap contains one simple directive—"start reading the instructions on the diskette in drive A." That's all MS-DOS needs to be up and running.

Right now you are looking at a blank, rather dreary screen. Let's put a little life into it.

Be sure you have the user's guide supplied by your manufacturer in a convenient location. Don't worry, you are not going to be cross-referenced to death. This book gives complete guidance for operating a "generic" MS-DOS system, but because not everyone has the same system, there may be slight differences in the wording or order of the messages which appear on the screen. If things seem a little different to you, just consult your user's guide.

If the Boot Fits . . .

To begin the booting up process, locate your *operating system diskette*. This will be labeled MS-DOS or some other variant of a DOS name. Since this diskette contains your operating system, it is the key to your computer's operation.

Next insert the diskette into disk drive A. If you have a question about "which end is up" on the diskette or "which drive is A," consult your user's guide. Every computer sage will recount his favorite story of trying to get something to work for hours, using all kinds of imaginable procedures, only to discover that the diskette was in wrong or was hiding in the wrong drive. Be sure and close the drive door after inserting the diskette; you can't get any information from a diskette unless the door is closed.

Check, steps one and two accomplished. Now you're ready to fire her up. But where's the on switch? This is another question for your user's guide, but the switch is *probably* on the side or back of your machine. Turn on the power and wait patiently.

It takes a few seconds for the machine to "wake up and stretch." Then, several things happen at once. You'll hear some whirring sounds as the cooling fan comes on and you may be startled by a short electronic "beep." Then a small line will start flashing on the screen. Good, this is the first sign of life! This line is the *cursor,* a small marker that indicates your place on the screen. Your cursor may or may not flash and it may have another shape besides an underline. More about the cursor in a moment.

Booting Checklist

1. FIND SYSTEM DISKETTE
2. LOCATE DRIVE A
3. INSERT DISKETTE
4. CLOSE DRIVE DOOR
5. TURN ON POWER
6. RELAX AND WAIT!

You will also notice the drive's indicator light (usually red) flashing on and off. You can hear the drive moving when the light is on. All of this is quite normal. Your machine is just doing some self-checking and getting ready to receive instructions. (If none of the above occurs after a minute or two, check to be sure the machine is plugged in.)

When the activity stops, there will be a message on your screen. It should read something like this:

```
Current date is Tues 1-01-1980   The date may be different.
Enter new date: __
```

Notice that the cursor is now after the word date. The cursor indicates the spot where the next incoming piece of information will appear on the screen. In this case, it means that when you type in a new date, it will be placed directly after the colon.

How Does That Data Get in There?

The computer is waiting for some information. Now is the moment of truth. You will use the keyboard to enter data into the computer. Sometimes your entry is in response to a request such as the "enter new date" statement. Sometimes *you* initiate the interaction with a request of your own.

Entering Data into the Machine

Understanding Instructions. At first, deciphering how, what, and when to enter information may seem mysterious. But there is no secret to deciphering the instructions in this book because herein lies your "official code breaker."

Symbol	Meaning
	This indicates a screen. Information appears inside this marker exactly as it appears on the screen.
`A>Format another? (Y/N)`	Information within the screen in black type is supplied by the computer.
`A>format b:`	Information within the screen in green type is supplied by you. When you type your entries be sure to include all punctuation and leave blank spaces where indicated.
< >	These brackets indicate a key on the keyboard (other than the letter or number keys).
<ENTER>	The <ENTER> key is your signal that you have finished typing in an entry. YOU MUST PRESS THE <ENTER> KEY BEFORE THE COMPUTER CAN RESPOND TO YOUR COMMANDS OR INSTRUCTIONS. The <ENTER> key may appear on your keyboard as <RETURN> or <↵ >.

Some Common Misconceptions.   To the computer, each key means a different character. You must not type the 1 (number one) if you really mean the l (lower-case L). The same is true of the 0 (number zero) and the O (uppercase O).

The spacebar on your computer does not simply move the cursor across the screen. It also sends a message to the computer—"Make this a blank space." If you want to move along a line, but not insert blank characters or erase existing characters, use the right arrow key <→>.

Correcting Mistakes.   Since you are just beginning your exploration of the computer, it's natural that you will make mistakes (especially if you're also new at typing!). So double-check your entries *before* you press the <ENTER> key. If you find a mistake just use the <BACKSPACE> key (it may look like this

<←>) to erase characters until you back up to the error. Then retype the entry. No white-out or smudged copies here!

If you can't get the keyboard to accept your data, or you've lost track of what is going on, just press the <Esc> (Escape) key. If all else fails, turn off the machine and take it from the top.

Take a moment to find these keys on your keyboard.

How Do You Set the Calendar and Clock?

Once you get the message to "enter new date" you have completed the "boot." This is the way the screen looks now:

```
Current date is Tues 1-01-1980
Enter new date: __
```

The date you see on the screen will not be today's date. Let's say that today is August 1, 1984. This is the new date you want to enter. You can enter the date in a variety of ways:

8-1-84
08-1-84
8/1/84
08/01/84

Whichever method you use to enter the date, the key thing here is to separate the parts of the date with hyphens or slashes. Notice that you don't enter the day of the week, just the numeric equivalents of the month, day, and year. Enter the date now:

```
Current date is Tues 1-01-1980
Enter new date: 8-1-84 <ENTER>
```

Immediately after you enter the date, MS-DOS returns the current time and asks you if you want to enter a new time:

```
Current time is 0:00:46.08
Enter new time: __
```

At this point, the computer is really in the Twilight Zone—no hours, no minutes. But "time stands still for no machine," so enter the current time now. Our current hypothetical time is 9:30 in the morning. Here are the various ways you could enter the time:

9:30:00.0
9:30:0
09:30:0
9:30

Your computer follows the international standard of the 24-hour clock. This means that the hours after midnight to noon are indicated by 0-12. After noon the hours go from 13-24 (midnight). You can enter the time according to the precise hours, minutes, seconds, and tens of seconds, but for most applications the hour and minutes suffice nicely. When entering the time, separate the hour, minutes, and seconds with a colon (:). If you do add the tens of seconds, they are preceded by a period. Now enter the time:

```
Current time is 0:00:46.08
Enter new time: 9:30 <ENTER>
```

Easy, fast, and precise! Your clock and calendar are now right on the mark. And you did very well with your first computer encounter! After a while, setting the date and time will become second nature to you.

The computer does not remember the date and time after you shut off the power, so you need to set the date and time each time you boot the machine. While this is sometimes inconvenient, it's a good idea to set the calendar and clock each time you start working, because the computer uses the date and time to keep track of the data you enter, add, or update. However, if you want to skip the date and time settings, just press the <ENTER> key in response to the new date and time requests.

Some computers have a clock/calendar which is set once and then reports the time and date automatically. If your system has this feature, you will not have to set the time and date at the beginning of each computer session.

Pilot To Control—Help!

What we have been describing is the ideal sequence of events when setting the time and date. But what happens if you follow the instructions (you think perfectly), and this message appears on the screen:

```
INVALID DATE or INVALID TIME
or
ok
```

There is nothing to worry about, just try the entry again. You probably put a period where you need a slash or some such. If you get the ok signal, you will need to boot the system again.

Boot Temperature (Cold Versus Warm)

When you insert the operating system diskette and then turn on the power, you are performing a "cold" boot, or starting the machine from a "power off" position. There is another kind of boot that occurs when you are already working on the machine (the power is on), but you want to start over again from the beginning. This is called a "warm" boot. You might perform a warm boot if you had entered the wrong date or had gotten the "ok" message described above. To warm boot the system, press down the <Ctrl> key, and while holding down <Ctrl>, press the <Alt> and <Del> keys. This brings you back to the "enter the date" message.

"COLD BOOT"

Your machine is turned off. Insert the
operating system diskette and turn on the
power.

"WARM BOOT"

Your machine is already in use. Press
the <Ctrl> <Alt> <Del> combination.

Cold boot versus warm boot.

You Are Now Entering MS-DOS Airspace

The date and time are your clearance, once they are set you are truly "in" the operating system. How do you know when MS-DOS is up and running and ready to receive commands from you?

After you enter the time your screen will look like this:

```
A>_
```

The capital letter A followed by the greater than symbol > is the MS-DOS *prompt* (some systems use a prompt which has the letter A followed by a colon, A:). A prompt tells you that the machine is waiting for you to enter some information. Notice that the cursor follows the prompt, indicating the location of the next entry.

Prompts vary with the program in use. While "A" is the DOS prompt, "ok" is the prompt for the BASIC programming language, and "*" is the prompt for the EDLIN program, a special part of the MS-DOS operating system. (You will learn to use EDLIN in Chapter 5.)

In response to the A> prompt, you are going to give MS-DOS your first *command*. Commands are nothing more than instructions to the operating system. They consist of short words or abbreviations that tell MS-DOS to perform specific actions. Right now, you want to find out what's on a diskette.

Who's on the Passenger List?

The DIR Command

use: displays a general diskette directory or lists the specific attributes of a single file

examples: dir
             dir command.com

The DIR command (short for DIRectory) lists information about *files* on a specific diskette. Files, or collections of related data, are the way MS-DOS keeps track of which information is stored where. All the files on your system diskette come ready-made from MS-DOS. You will learn how to create your own files in Chapter 6. You use the DIR command to see the names of all the files that are on a diskette, or to find out if a single file is located on a particular diskette.

Listing all the Files

Since our system diskette is already in drive A, let's use the DIR command to see what files are on this diskette. When you enter a command you can use either upper- or lowercase letters (don't forget to include all punctuation and blank spaces). Enter this command now:

```
A>dir <ENTER>
```

MS-DOS responds with a listing of the files. But if you are viewing the "typical" operating system diskette, you may be feeling a slight panic. Did the entire screen fill up and then move on quickly to another screen? No one can read anything that fast! What do you do now?

Stop the Action!

There is a simple explanation for this phenomenon. MS-DOS presents information to you one screen at a time. This is fine if the diskette contains only a few files; after they are listed the display stops. But when a diskette contains many files, they cannot fit on the screen at one time, and the display will *scroll*. Scrolling means that as the screen is filled with information, new data is added to the bottom of the display as old data rolls off the top. This does make it very difficult to read. However, there is a simple way to freeze the screen and stop this scrolling action.

To stop scrolling you press and hold down the <Ctrl> key and then press the S key. Release both keys together. In some systems you stop scrolling by holding down <Ctrl> and pressing the <Num Lock> key.

Keeping Everything Under Control

The <Ctrl> key used to stop scrolling is the same <Ctrl> key which is part of the <Ctrl> <Alt> <Del> combination used to perform a warm boot. You will find that the <Ctrl> key is a device of many uses. It is never used alone, but always in conjunction with other keys on the keyboard. In some ways, <Ctrl> is like a master toggle switch. When used with another key, it changes the message that key sends to the computer. Whenever you use <Ctrl> you must press and hold down this key while pressing another key or keys. All keys are released together.

Try using the DIR command to list the diskette contents again. If your display is more than one screen long, freeze the scrolling action by using the <Ctrl> S combination:

```
A>dir <ENTER>
   <Ctrl> S
```

Press any key (<ENTER> is a good one to use) to begin the scrolling again. When the display is finished, the screen will look similar to this:

```
SORT      EXE       1280     3-08-83     12:00P
FIND      EXE       5888     3-08-83     12:00P
MORE      COM        384     3-08-83     12:00P
BASIC     COM      16256     3-08-83     12:00P
BASICA    COM      25984     3-08-83     12:00P
        23 File(s)        31232 bytes free

A>
```

The exact names and numbers do not matter, and may vary according to the diskette included in your system. The information on the screen describes the files that are on the operating system diskette. Let's look at the pattern in which the files are listed:

```
        Volume in drive A has no label
        Directory of A:\

    filename ext    size          date         time
    COMMAND   COM   17664      3-08-83      12:00P
    ANSI      SYS    1664      3-08-83      12:00P
    FORMAT    COM    6016      3-08-83      12:00P
    CHKDSK    COM    6400      3-08-83      12:00P
    SYS       COM    1408      3-08-83      12:00P
    DISKCOPY  COM    2444      3-08-83      12:00P
    DISKCOMP  COM    2074      3-08-83      12:00P
    COMP      COM    2523      3-08-83      12:00P
    EDLIN     COM    4608      3-08-83      12:00P
    MODE      COM    3139      3-08-83      12:00P
    FDISK     COM    6177      3-08-83      12:00P
    BACKUP    COM    3687      3-08-83      12:00P
    RESTORE   COM    4003      3-08-83      12:00P
    PRINT     COM    4608      3-08-83      12:00P
    RECOVER   COM    2304      3-08-83      12:00P
    ASSIGN    COM     896      3-08-83      12:00P
    TREE      COM    1513      3-08-83      12:00P
    GRAPHICS  COM     789      3-08-83      12:00P
    SORT      EXE    1280      3-08-83      12:00P
    FIND      EXE    5888      3-08-83      12:00P
    MORE      COM     384      3-08-83      12:00P
    BASIC     COM   16256      3-08-83      12:00P
    BASICA    COM   25984      3-08-83      12:00P
        23 File(s)        31232 bytes free

A>
```

If you are looking at the first page of the directory listing, you may see a short statement about the *volume label*. Ignore this for now. This is a mystery which will be unraveled in Chapter 7.

The body of the listing is divided into five separate columns. Column 1 gives us the name of the file, for example, SORT, FIND, MORE, BASIC. This name identifies the contents of the file. Column 2 is an extension of the file's name. EXE and COM tell us what type of file these are. Pay no attention to these particulars right now. The science and art of filenaming is detailed in Chapter 6.

Column 3 tells us how big the file is. File size is measured in bytes, so the SORT file takes up 1280 bytes on the diskette. Columns 4 and 5 tell us the date and time that the file was last updated (this is the type of information that is supplied when you set the time and date at the beginning of a computer session).

Finally, MS-DOS performs a little housekeeping chore. It reports the total number of files on the diskette and the space available on the diskette for new files. This information will be very useful to you later, when you are deciding if a file will fit on a certain diskette.

That's a lot of information from one small three letter command!

Notice that when MS-DOS is finished performing the DIR command, it returns you to the operating system. You know this has happened when you see the DOS prompt A>.

Listing a Specific File

In addition to listing all the files on a diskette, DIR can also tell you if a specific file is on a particular diskette. To get this information enter the command followed by a "filename." Although you already know the contents of your system diskette, let's assume that you are trying to find a file named "COMMAND.COM". Enter the DIR command, leave a blank space, and then enter the name of the file:

```
A> dir command.com <ENTER>
```

MS-DOS replies:

```
    Volume in drive A has no label
    Directory of A:\

COMMAND    COM    17664    3-08-83    12:00P
        1 File(s)        31232 bytes free
```

And there it is—all of the same information listed in columns one through five, as they describe this particular file.

If the file you request is not on the diskette, MS-DOS returns this message:

```
File not found
```

Sorry, try again. Either you never put the file on this diskette or you are looking at a different diskette than you thought.

Well, now you are reaping the fruits of your labors (either a DIR of the entire diskette or a DIR of the COMMAND.COM file). But how do you remove this information from the screen? Our next command provides the answer.

Starting with a Clean Slate

The CLS Command

use: clears all the information from the screen

example: cls

As you use your computer more and more, you soon realize that a lot of the information you display is for "your eyes only." In other words, you don't need to save the information after you have seen it. And with mistakes and changes of mind, you can fill up a screen pretty quickly. For instance, in the previous use of the DIR command, you displayed all the files on your system diskette. You don't really need this information once you have looked at the listing. You have no special reason to save it. The CLS (CLear Screen) command is a handy way of getting rid of all the stuff on the screen that you are tired of looking at. (The CLS command isn't available on MS-DOS Version 1.0 and 1.1.) Try using CLS now to empty the screen:

```
A>cls <ENTER>
```

Like magic the screen is cleared. After you execute the CLS command, the cursor waits for the next entry in the upper left-hand corner of the screen. This is sometimes called the cursor's "home" position.

CLS affects only the information *currently on the screen*. It does nothing to data in memory or to information stored on diskettes. The corollary is that it also saves nothing. Use CLS only when you don't need the information on the screen.

Okay, time to take a breather. You've really come a long way in one short session! In this chapter you've learned how to insert your system diskette into the disk drive, and how to perform a cold and a warm boot. You've learned some simple rules for entering data into the machine, and gotten your "hands wet" by setting the calendar and clock in your system and entering your first MS-DOS commands. The DIR command allowed you to display the listing for a diskette and <Ctrl> S showed you how to freeze that display. The CLS command cleaned up your screen when you were finished looking at the displayed information. And you thought this was going to be tough!

In the next chapter we are going to take a closer look at one piece of computer technology that helped spawn the personal computer revolution, the floppy disk!

4

System Insurance

4 System Insurance

There is a precaution that most of us take as a matter of course whenever we acquire something we want to protect or safeguard. We take out insurance. Whether for your health, your house, or that new car you have waited so long for, you automatically insure it. And then, if the unexpected happens, you are protected.

Well, your newly acquired operating system diskette falls into the category of "valuable things you would be lost without." The sad truth is: no operating system diskette, no computer operation. In this chapter you will learn how to take out this insurance at no additional cost to you (except the cost of a floppy diskette). In other words, you will make a *backup* copy of your operating system diskette. By using this backup in your everyday computing, you always have the original to fall back on if your diskette should suffer damage or you "misplace" it.

It is staggering to think of how much information is stored on that one magnetically coated piece of plastic. Detailed instructions about how the computer is to receive input, manage files, deliver output, and operate its equipment, it's all there on this one diskette. In addition, one small diskette still has room to store programming languages and maybe a utility program or two.

Before you actually insure this precious commodity, let's take a closer look at what makes up a diskette.

Diskettes and Disk Drives

Just as the size, speed, and capabilities of computer hardware have undergone a remarkable technological evolution in the last three decades, so have the methods for storing the programs and data the computer needs to operate.

As mentioned in Chapter 2, earnest computer users of the 50s and 60s used the primitive storage method of "punch cards." These cards, 80 columns wide, were stored in long oversized boxes. Transporting "programs" involved struggles with many unwieldy boxes, which were subject to agonizing rearrangement when dropped, or worse—"bent, folded, or mutilated."

Gradually, paper tape and cards were replaced by plastic-coated "disks." By imbedding information in the surface coating material on these disks, users could store much larger quantities of data and in a much safer way. Once the information was on the diskette, it could only be lost through mishandling or intentional erasing.

The first type of diskettes were 8″ in diameter. Because they were flexible, they were termed *floppy diskettes*. Constructed of thin, plastic mylar and surfaced with a magnetic coating, you could store information on only one side of the diskette. Typically, the 8″ diskette held 50-100K bytes of information.

"Floppies" rapidly got smaller and became capable of holding more and more information. Modification to the reading "heads" of the disk drive allowed both sides of the diskette to hold data. Today, "minifloppies" (5¼" in diameter) are used for most systems that operate using MS-DOS.

The capacity of 5¼" diskettes varies according to their design. Some diskettes record on one side (single sided), some use both sides to store data (double sided). In addition, the amount of information on the diskette depends on the density of the storage. Some diskettes are single density. Others achieve twice as

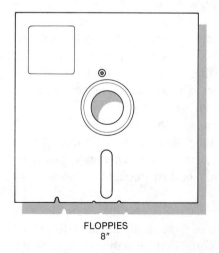
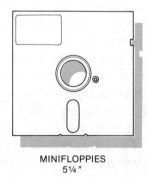

FLOPPIES
8"

MINIFLOPPIES
5¼"

MICROFLOPPIES
3½"

Diskette evolution.

much storage by packing data in double density. The "average" double-sided, double-density diskette can contain about 362K bytes of information. (Fixed disks with many, many times more storage are different beasts altogether and are discussed in Chapter 11.)

Recently, a new, even smaller media has arrived on the disk scene. These "microfloppies" are approximately 3½″ in diameter. They are held in a rigid, rather than flexible, sleeve. Microdisks are still in the process of standardization. Currently, 3½″ disks utilize only one side for data storage. However, given the direction of prior disk development, it is likely that double-sided microdisks with increased densities will soon be available.

How data gets put on diskettes is covered later in this chapter. For now, the only thing you need to know about your diskettes is what *type* your computer uses. Check your owner's manual for the specific types of diskettes you should buy.

The Nature of Diskettes

Whatever their size, "sidedness," or density, all diskettes have several features in common. This discussion will describe the most common features found on 5¼″ floppy diskettes.

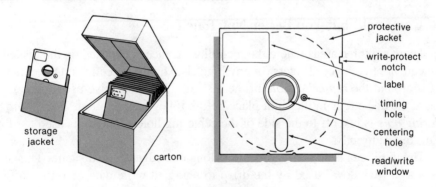

Features of diskettes.

Diskettes usually come stored in convenient boxes (save these for storing your diskettes). Inside the carton, each diskette is nestled inside a paper envelope. This is the diskette's *storage jacket*. It's a good idea to put this paper jacket on the diskette whenever you're not using it.

The diskette is completely enclosed inside a square plastic *protective jacket*. The actual shape of the diskette is round. This protective jacket is permanent and should never be removed. In fact you won't be able to remove it unless you are using a sharp instrument like a knife or scissors, or perhaps the teeth of an errant dog! If the diskette does not appear square in shape, something dreadful has happened to the protective jacket (and undoubtedly to any information which was on the diskette).

You Can Look, but You Better Not Touch

There are three areas where the recording surface is exposed on the diskette. Take care *not* to put your fingers (or anything else) on these sections. One exposed area is around the *centering hole* of the diskette. The disk drive uses this area to be sure the diskette is in the right place before it begins operation. The *timing* or *indexing hole* is just off to the side of the centering hole. This too is used to align the diskette correctly.

The third area is an oblong opening along one edge of the diskette. This area serves as a "window" used by the drive to read and write data onto the surface of the diskette. As the diskette revolves, the special *heads* within the disk drive

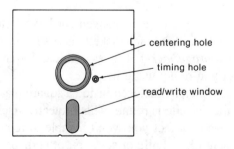

Exposed surfaces.

(just like the heads on a tape recorder) code the magnetic surface with information that contains the pattern of your data. It is especially important to keep this window free of all dirt or dust. Imperfections in this window can be transferred to the drive heads and damage your drives, as well as your diskettes.

Righting the "Write" Stuff

Along one edge of the diskette, you will see a distinct square cut-out indentation. This is the *write-protect notch*. A very clever design feature, this small space may save you from a fate worse than death—erasing vital information by inadvertently writing over it.

New information can overwrite, or erase, previous information. But before the computer writes to a diskette, it checks this notch. If the notch is *covered,* the diskette is "write-protected," that is, it cannot receive new data. If the notch is *open,* the diskette is fair game for both reading and writing.

When you want to make sure that the contents of a diskette are not altered, cover this notch with one of the *write-protect tabs* included in your box of purchased diskettes (there will be several oblong tabs stuck on one sheet; they are usually silver or black). These pieces of adhesive foil or paper seal off the notch and prevent any new information from being written to the diskette.

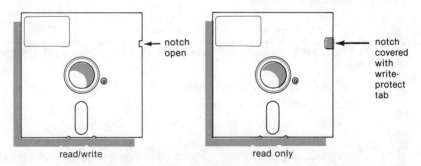

Write-protect notch.

You may notice that some diskettes, especially those containing application programs, have no write-protect notch. Another form of free insurance for you! If you can't write to the diskette, you don't run the risk of altering or destroying the program.

Better Living through Labeling

Also in your carton of purchased diskettes, you will find a packet of adhesive labels (they come in many colors and usually have lines on them). These are *content labels,* a means of identifying each diskette. These labels can save you mountains of frustration. Without labeling, most diskettes look distressingly alike, as you may discover late one evening as you sit among piles of unidentifiable diskettes looking for the one you "put down for just a minute." (See Commandment 7 following.) How much information you put on these labels is up to you, but it should be clear enough so that you'll know what's on your diskette when you pick it up next month, or next year.

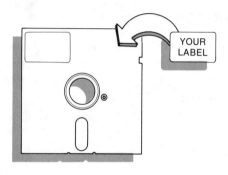

Labeling.

All this talk of "do this" and "don't do that" may have you wondering if you will ever have the courage to pick up a diskette, let alone use it in your computer. But fear not ye of little faith, a concise tract to peaceful coexistence with your diskettes follows.

The Ten Commandments of Disk Handling and Usage

1. Thou shalt not rest heavy objects upon thy diskette surfaces. Such objects include reference books, instruction manuals, and the omnipresent elbow.

2. Thou shalt not eat, drink, smoke, nor comb thy hair around thy diskettes. These seemingly simple activities of daily life can cause great havoc when deposited upon the surface of a diskette. Thou shalt always be on guard against the "coffee cup demon."

3. Thou shalt not bend, staple, paper clip, or mutilate thy diskettes whether by rough handling or improper storage.

4. Thou shalt protect diskettes from the common forces of creation. This encompasses the peril of destruction by sunlight or exposure to acts of high temperature and/or humidity.

5. Neither X-ray machines (including those at the airport inquisition), telephones, nor any other source of magnetic energy (beware the mag-

netic paper clip dispenser) let come near thy diskettes. These "fields of force" can wreck havoc with thy diskettes' good intentions.

6. Keep thy fingers to thyself. Thou shalt handle thy diskettes by the edges only, and gently.

7. Acknowledge the individuality of thy diskettes by proper labeling. When transcribing said labels, use only a felt-tip pen, for pencils and ballpoints do damage thy diskettes. Unlabeled diskettes carrying precious information have been known to succumb to the destructive prowess of the FORMAT command.

8. Store thy diskettes with honor. Specifically, refrain from resting thy diskettes on their sides, or crowding them too closely into a closed space.

9. When not in use, clothe thy diskettes properly. Thou shalt always return thy diskettes to their storage jackets.

10. Know that the responsibility for thy diskettes rests upon thy shoulders. Diskette loyalty and performance is directly related to thy loving care and devotion.

How Is That Data Stored on the Diskette?

MS-DOS is a careful and efficient manager, so when it stores information on a diskette it does so in an orderly, logical way. Before any information can be put on a diskette, the diskette must first be prepared using the FORMAT command (discussed later in this chapter). Your blank diskette, fresh from the box, is like a newly paved running track, one large, unmarked surface. The first thing that FORMAT does is divide this area into specific *tracks*. The tracks run in concentric circles around the diskette, much like the painted lanes that mark boundaries for runners on a running track.

The tracks are divided into small sections called *sectors*. This makes storage and retrieval of your data faster and more efficient because MS-DOS knows just what track and sector holds each file. This is equivalent to knowing a friend's house number; it makes finding him more efficient than wandering aimlessly up and down the street. The amount of data stored in a sector is dependent upon your computer system. Most diskettes used with MS-DOS divide the diskette into 8 or 9 sectors per track. Each sector can hold either 512 or 1024 bytes.

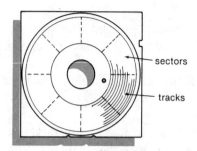

Tracks and sectors.

The first section of the first track on every diskette is reserved for storage of the operating system. Thereafter, as data is written to the diskette, it is stored on a first-come, first-served basis. You do not need to remember the order in which you store data on the diskette, MS-DOS keeps track of that for you.

Getting the Diskette Ready to Be Used

It's easy to prepare your diskettes for use. Don't let this new challenge make you nervous. After all, you already know how to handle diskettes, and how they go into your disk drive (remember how well you executed the DIR command). But a little planning can make things easier for you as you perform this procedure. Be sure and have the following tools ready:

the computer, up and running
your computer instruction manual
the system diskette
several new, blank diskettes

The instructions for the following MS-DOS commands are given in terms of the "typical" MS-DOS system. Do you have a typical system? To find out, answer the following question.

How Many Drives Do You Have?

When asking questions and giving responses to commands, MS-DOS assumes that you have two disk drives, "A" and "B". Operating with at least two drives is the most efficient method for MS-DOS because it simplifies transferring information from one diskette to the other, and makes giving instructions easier. With two drives, MS-DOS can easily differentiate where the information is "coming from" and where the information is "going to."

The operating system is quite set in its ways on this point. So much so that even if you have a single drive, MS-DOS *pretends* you have two. It always issues instructions in terms of drive "A" and drive "B". How can single drive owners use this system? Well, you just have to participate in some chicanery yourself.

One easy way to do this is to think of your diskettes as "drives." That is, one diskette represents drive "A" and the second represents drive "B". Then when the displays tells you to do "x, y, and z" with the diskette in drive A, you use the first diskette. When you need to do "x, y, and z" with the diskette in drive B, you remove the first diskette and insert the second diskette before

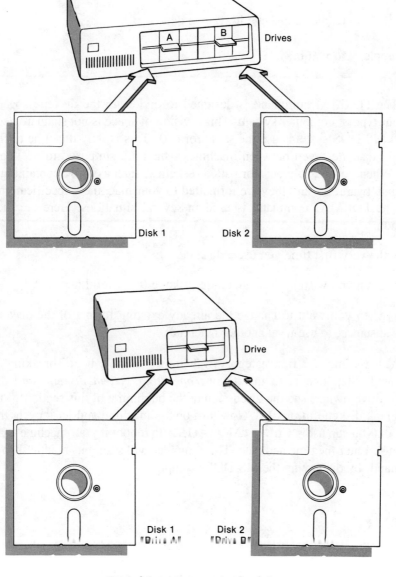

Two drives versus single drive.

performing the action. Both the operating system and you are happy and no one is any the wiser.

With these preliminaries out of the way, you're ready to prepare some new diskettes. To accomplish this, you will call upon the FORMAT command.

Filling in the Blank Spaces

The FORMAT Command

use: readies a diskette to receive data

example: format b:

The FORMAT command is designed to divide up the diskette specifically for your type of computer system. This division of space is not standardized (i.e., not all MS-DOS systems use the same format). This is why it can be difficult to "swap" diskettes even between machines which are supposed to be "compatible." When you buy already formatted diskettes, such as those containing application software, be sure they are formatted to your machine's specifications.

The FORMAT command is used in several situations. Here are the most common:

- the very first time you use a diskette

- when you wish to erase an entire diskette (be careful here)

- when you want to change the already existing format of the diskette (for instance, to use it on another machine)

You fit into the first category right now, so let's begin breaking in this command. Step one is to insert your *operating system diskette* into drive A (single-drive owners see the discussion at the beginning of this section). Put your new blank diskette in drive B. Now turn on the machine and let it cycle through the boot (you can use <Ctrl> <Alt> <Del> to reboot if your machine is already running). Enter the time and date. The computer will signal its readiness to accept commands by displaying the MS-DOS prompt:

```
A>
```

Now you are going to tell the operating system to FORMAT the diskette in drive B. YOU MUST INCLUDE THE LETTER B IN YOUR COMMAND OR ELSE YOU MIGHT DESTROY YOUR SYSTEM DISKETTE. Enter the command:

```
A>format b: <ENTER>    Be sure to include the space between the
                       command and the drive specifier, and the colon
                       after the letter b.
```

Now watch the screen. It answers your command with this response:

```
Insert new diskette for drive B:
and strike any key when ready
```

Since you have already put a new, blank diskette in drive B, you can press any key.

The drive will click and whirr, and the indicator light will go on and off. Do not interrupt this process, just let the machine do its work. The operating system lets you know what is going on by displaying this message:

```
Formatting...
```

Once the formatting is completed, it tells you this also:

```
Formatting...Format complete

   362496 bytes total disk space
   362496 bytes available on disk

Format another (Y/N)?
```

Let's take a moment to look at the messages MS-DOS is giving you. First you are told that the formatting of the disk has been completed. Then the total number of bytes on the disk is given. Since formatting has not put any information on the diskette, but has only divided up the space, the amount of total disk space and the amount available on the disk are the same.

You must now make a decision. Do you want to format any additional diskettes? If you answer "Y", you will be instructed to insert another diskette in drive B. It's a good idea to format several diskettes at a time. Then, when you desperately need a diskette to put the crowning touches on some masterful project, you won't have to stop, insert your system diskette, and then prepare the diskette. As long as you're here, go ahead and format several diskettes now.

Good for you! Everything is moving along smoothly and you now have several pristine diskettes eagerly awaiting use. When you're tired of formatting, just answer "N" to the "Format another" question and you will be returned to the MS-DOS prompt.

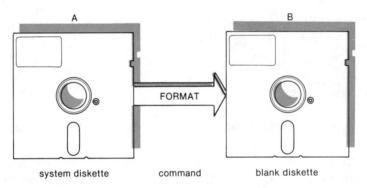

The FORMAT command.

Signed, Sealed, and Delivered

But you're not quite finished. Be sure and *label* those diskettes. This label can be quite short or rather long, just so its meaning is clear to you. One simple label consists of the letter F, or the word "formatted," followed by the date. This leaves lots of room for you to fill in the contents of the diskette as you store information on it.

One note of caution in using the FORMAT command. When you tell MS-DOS to format, you are indicating that this is a new, blank diskette. FORMAT, then, ignores any information already on a diskette; it merrily lays down new track and sector divisions. This can be useful if you want to erase an entire diskette. Just use FORMAT and *voila!* Everything is gone. But naturally this situation can also backfire. If you FORMAT a diskette that contains something you really want, or desperately need, there is no tomorrow. The data is gone.

This only reiterates the importance of labeling all diskettes. Keep this fact in mind whenever you use the FORMAT command: FORMAT TREATS EACH DISKETTE AS BLANK, IT WILL ERASE ANY INFORMATION ON THE DISKETTE.

Occasionally, when you format a diskette, you will receive a different message. It will look something like this:

```
Bad sector on track xxx
or
xxxxx bytes in bad sector
```

If this message appears, do not continue to use the diskette. There is probably some manufacturing fault with the diskette (and possibly with the entire carton of diskettes). Return these diskettes to your dealer and request a refund or replacement.

Writing the Insurance Policy

Now, before you do anything else, you are going to make that insurance copy of your system diskette. This copy will be an exact duplicate of the original diskette. You do not want to add or delete any information. Whenever you want to copy an *entire diskette,* produce an identical twin as it were, you use the DISKCOPY command.

The DISKCOPY Command

use: makes a duplicate of an entire diskette

example: diskcopy a: b:

Normally, before transferring any information to a diskette, you must prepare it using FORMAT. But in the case of the DISKCOPY command, the exception proves the rule. DISKCOPY *automatically* formats the diskette as it makes the duplicate copy. Since this is true, the same precautions exist when using this command: DISKCOPY ERASES ANY PREVIOUS INFORMATION ON THE DISKETTE.

It's important to distinguish between DISKCOPY and COPY (an MS-DOS command introduced in Chapter 6). DISKCOPY can only make an exact copy of *all the files on the diskette.* When you want to copy only part of the files on a diskette, you use the COPY command.

DISKCOPY versus COPY	
DISKCOPY	**COPY**
automatically formats diskette copies entire diskette	needs a formatted diskette copies only designated files

Now let's make DISKCOPY jump through its hoops. If it's not already there, put your system diskette in drive A. Insert an unformatted, blank diskette in drive B.

Before you enter this command, take a close look at the exact wording of the example:

```
diskcopy a: b:
```

This DISKCOPY command tells MS-DOS to copy the entire contents *from* the diskette in drive A *to* the diskette in drive B. Of course, the instructions are in a kind of shorthand so this is probably not readily apparent to you. BE SURE YOU ENTER THE COMMAND IN THIS EXACT ORDER. OTHERWISE YOU MAY ERASE YOUR ENTIRE SYSTEM DISKETTE.

How can this happen? Well, as DISKCOPY transfers the information it wipes out anything previously on the diskette. So when you are using this command you must be sure to clearly indicate where the information is coming from and where it is going to.

Clarifying the Beneficiary

The diskette that holds the original information is your *source diskette*. It contains the information you want to copy. In this case the source diskette is your system diskette, currently in drive A.

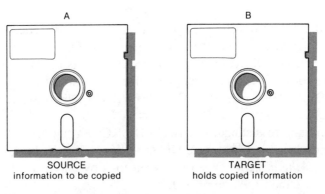

A   B

SOURCE
information to be copied

TARGET
holds copied information

Source and target diskettes.

The diskette that receives the copy is your *target diskette*. It is the destination of the information you are copying. Your target diskette (as yet empty) is currently in drive B.

It's wise to become familiar with these terms because they are used in the instructions MS-DOS uses to perform copying commands. You'll see an example of this now as you execute DISKCOPY:

```
A>diskcopy a: b: <ENTER>    Include the blank spaces and colons.
```

MS-DOS gives you a reminder:

```
Insert source diskette in drive A

Insert target diskette in drive B

Strike any key when ready
```

Well, that couldn't be much clearer. You already have the source and target diskettes in place, so press any key.

The operating system now performs the same sequence of events that accompanied the FORMAT command, with the added bonus of copying the contents of the diskette at the same time. Again the drives will whirr and the indicator lights will flash on and off. When the light under drive A is lit, information is being read from the system diskette. When the light under drive B comes on, information is being written to this diskette. DO NOT ATTEMPT TO OPEN THE DRIVE DOORS OR REMOVE ANY DISKETTES WHILE THIS COMMAND IS IN OPERATION.

During this process, this message will be on the screen:

```
Copying 9 sectors per track, 2 side(s)
```

Depending on the type of diskette your system uses, your message may read a bit differently (it may have 8 sectors or copy on only one side). But in any case, MS-DOS tells you when the DISKCOPY command has finished copying the diskette:

```
Copy complete

Copy another (Y/N)?
```

At this point you are offered an option. In the same way that you can use FORMAT repeatedly without retyping the command, you can also use DISK-COPY to make more than one duplicate of the source diskette. If you answer "Y" to MS-DOS's query, you are instructed to insert a new target diskette in drive B and start the copying process with a keystroke. If you answer "N" you are returned to the system prompt. Here is a chance for you to exert your individuality. If you want to be doubly protected, make an extra copy of your "insurance" diskette. If you want to live dangerously, don't!

Now you are all set. You have taken out an insurance policy on your system diskette (properly labeled, of course). You can take your original system diskette and store it in a dry, safe place. Keep your backup system diskette and your newly formatted diskettes handy, you will need them in the very next chapter.

DISKCOPY is the first MS-DOS command you have encountered that requires the use of two diskettes, one in each drive. Many MS-DOS commands rely on this kind of "transfer" of information from one diskette to another. It is important that you understand exactly how MS-DOS identifies which drive to find the information "on" and which drive to transfer the information "to." You inform MS-DOS as to which is the "source" and which is the "target" through the use of drive indicators.

A Written Guarantee

After you complete a command, MS-DOS returns you to the system prompt:

```
A>
```

You are now back under the control of the MS-DOS operating system, that is, MS-DOS is ready for your next command. Besides being the system prompt, the "A" symbol gives you another important piece of information. It informs you that the system is working off the A drive. It expects that any information you request or store will be on this drive. So this "A" is also a *drive indicator.*

⊛ In order to keep track of itself, MS-DOS uses the concept of "current" drive. The current drive is the one represented by the drive indicator. This is also called the "default" drive because, unless you tell it otherwise, MS-DOS will always look for information or store information on the current drive.

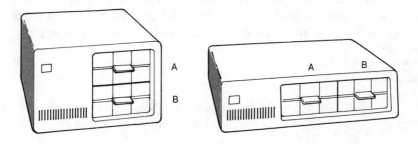

Take, for example, the DIR command. You want a listing of the diskette in drive A. You ask for this information by entering the command, followed by a drive indicator. Drive indicators in commands are separated from the command by a space and must be followed by a colon:

```
A>dir a: <ENTER>
```

This command produces a listing of all the files on the diskette in drive A. But you may be mumbling to yourself, *"That's not the way I got a listing of the system diskette."* You are absolutely right. This is how you entered the DIR command in Chapter 3:

```
A>dir <ENTER>
```

You did not include any drive indicator. These two versions of the DIR command produce the same listings because of the "default" feature of MS-DOS. The A system prompt tells you that A is the current drive, therefore when you enter a command without any drive indicator it lists the files on the diskette in the current, or A, drive.

This default feature is very handy when you are working extensively with one diskette. But it does have its drawbacks. You can cause some pretty weird and unwanted file changes if you neglect to include a drive indicator in a command. Since it does no harm to include a drive indicator, when in doubt *write it into the command*. Even if the operation only involves the current drive, it doesn't do any harm to include the default indicator in your command. Specifying drive indicators is always a good idea when you are transferring information from one diskette to another, just as an extra measure of protection.

You can issue commands to be performed on the diskette in other drives without changing the current drive. Suppose you had your system diskette in drive A and a diskette holding some data files in drive B. You want to see a directory of the data files. To do this you include the drive indicator in the command:

```
A>dir b: <ENTER>    The command is followed by a blank space, then the
                    drive indicator followed by a colon.
```

The screen displays the listing of the files on the diskette in drive B. After the listing you will be returned to the system prompt.

```
A>
```

The current drive is still A because you have only taken a "peek" at the files on the diskette in drive B. When you issue your next command, MS-DOS will look for the information or write the information to the diskette in drive A, as this is still your current drive.

> **Current Drive**
>
> The A> prompt indicates the current drive.

There will come a time when you will be working extensively with the diskette in drive B. When this is the case, it can become a bit inconvenient to keep including the drive indicator in every command, but there is a simple solution—change the current drive. To make drive B the current drive, just type in the drive indicator in response to the system prompt:

```
A>b: <ENTER>
```

The new current drive will then appear as the system prompt:

```
B>
```

Don't get confused, this is still the MS-DOS *system prompt,* it does not mean that MS-DOS is not operating. It's just that your definition of system prompt has expanded. The MS-DOS system prompt is now the indicator of the current drive followed by >. So both A> and B> are the MS-DOS system prompt.

Now that you have changed the current drive, what would be the result of the following command?

```
B>dir <ENTER>
```

If you answered *"A listing of the files on the diskette in drive B,"* give yourself two gold stars. Since B is now the current drive, and you did not include a drive indicator in the command, MS-DOS automatically performs the command on the diskette in drive B.

If you are still a bit confused about when to include a drive indicator, think of it this way. The computer can only do what you tell it to. Including drive indicators is like making a will, you can only be sure the goodies go to the right recipients if you make your wishes known (preferably by writing them down). If you tell MS-DOS that drive A is the current drive, it will return to that drive after every command *until you tell it differently.* It will also perform the entered command on the data in the current drive *unless you tell it to go to another diskette.* Be patient with the computer, it does many things quickly, but in reasoning abilities (or mind-reading abilities) it rates a fat zero!

To return to A as the current drive, enter the drive indicator in response to the B prompt:

```
B>a: <ENTER>
```

The current drive is again A:

```
A>
```

As you become more familiar with other MS-DOS commands, the significance and use of drive indicators will become clearer. This will be especially true as you move into more advanced MS-DOS commands in Chapter 6.

This completes the sales pitch from Mutual of MS-DOS. The theme of this chapter has been protecting yourself. This includes using and handling your diskettes wisely (it is your data!) and making sure you backup your original system diskette (it's your computer!). In addition, you have moved into the realm of actually "doing-something-with-a-diskette computing." You've used FORMAT to prepare your diskettes and DISKCOPY to make your insurance copy. Finally, you have begun to see more of the inner operations of MS-DOS by learning the basics of source and target diskettes and the current drive indicator.

5

Minding Your E's and Q's

5 Minding Your E's and Q's

Computers, no matter what their fancy names or reputed powers, are simply machines to organize information. This is also the purpose of software packages and programming languages; they are tools to help you arrange, classify, and use your data. But before you can use your computer for this task, you have to get the data in there.

Most of the information you enter into the computer is in the form of "text" or combinations of numbers, letters, and punctuation marks. MS-DOS keeps track of data by placing it into *files*. (You were introduced to files when you used the DIR command in Chapter 3.) These files, or groups of related data, are the meat and potatoes of using your computer. MS-DOS is a very efficient file organizer. You will learn how to name files and give MS-DOS commands to manage your files in Chapter 6.

But first you must learn how to create files. Included in the MS-DOS operating system is a special program named EDLIN. EDLIN is a text editor and its sole purpose is to help you create and edit files.

What Is an Editor?

EDLIN belongs to that category of computer software tools called *text editors*. Editors are used to create new files and add, delete, or modify text in existing files. In addition, editors can move text around inside a file or transfer information from one file to another.

There are two different types of editors, full screen editors and line editors. A *full screen editor* displays files so that the entire screen is filled with text (usually 23 lines at a time as this is the capacity of most personal computer monitors). Full screen editors are also called "word-processing programs." Each full screen is like a window, displaying a specific section of your entire file. Getting around in a full screen editor is quite simple. You have complete freedom of movement with your cursor, and you move from window to window with one or two keystrokes. To make changes in the text, you type directly into the window.

EDLIN, however, is a *line editor* (EDit LINes). Line editors are more limited than full screen editors and a bit more difficult to use. Each line of text is handled separately. Every line of text is identified by a line number. You use these line numbers to create your own "window."

One time-consuming part of using a line editor is that before you can perform any command, you must define the exact location where the operation is to occur. Then you enter instructions to move to this section and display the specified part of the text document. Only then can the editing changes be made.

Actually, using a line editor is not as complicated as it sounds, but these extra steps can slow you down and be frustrating until you are familiar with the

Two Types of Editors

Full Screen Editor	Line Editor
Displays entire screen	Displays designated block of lines
Edits anywhere on screen	Edits within one line
Sophisticated editing features	Limited set of commands
Adds special characters	Uses ASCII code
Long loading time	Built-in and compact
May use lots of memory	Doesn't take up much space
Can be expensive	Free with MS-DOS
Good for large files	Good for small editing jobs

EDLIN commands. If most of your work on the computer will be with large files, you should consider purchasing a word-processing program. For smaller jobs, EDLIN does just fine!

Safety in Numbers

One nice touch to the EDLIN editor is that it comes with a built-in safety device, for which you will thank the designers of EDLIN more than once during your computing experience. This feature is the automatic creation of a backup file whenever you modify an EDLIN file. This backup has the same name and contents as your text file, but is identifiable by a three letter addition to the filename. Not surprisingly, this extension is *.BAK*. When you list your files using the DIR command, you will see these "insurance" files listed with the .BAK extension:

```
Volume in drive A has no label
Directory of A:\

BILLS    TXT   46976   3-08-83   12:00P
SCORES   TXT    4608   3-08-83   12:00P
LETTERS  TXT   33920   3-08-83   12:00P
```

```
BILLS     BAK    45568   3-08-83   12:00P
SCORES    BAK     1408   3-08-83   12:00P
LETTERS   BAK    33792   3-08-83   12:00P
          6 File(s) 193024 bytes free
```

Backup files are essential to help you recover data if a problem occurs while you are in the middle of an editing session.

Imagine that you have worked long and hard to create a file and are just about ready to call it quits. But horror of horrors, due to some massive use of air-conditioners in the next state, you experience a power "black out." Of course, your computer goes off, and with it goes all of the changes and modifications you have been patiently entering for the last hour (they were in transient RAM memory). Well, EDLIN can't miraculously recover those changes, but it can help you "cut your losses." Because your original file still exists in the .BAK version, you will lose only the modifications entered during this current editing session.

EDLIN also has another built-in safety feature. It won't let you edit a file with a .BAK extension. If you could get into the backup files and randomly make changes to this last version, you wouldn't have that pristine copy when you needed it. To use a backup file, you must first give the file a new name, removing the .BAK designation. (You'll learn how to do this using the RENAME command in Chapter 6.) Once the file is no longer the backup, you can begin the editing process all over again (sigh).

What's in a Backup File?

An EDLIN .BAK file contains:
a duplicate version of the latest text in a file not including changes made in the current editing session.

Use a .BAK file:
whenever you lose the contents of an EDLIN file. You must first rename or remove the file extension.

Of course, if anything happens to your diskette, your insurance is cancelled because both the original and backup files are stored on the same diskette. It's a good practice to have "reserve" copies of your files on separate diskettes (the COPY command in Chapter 6 explains how to do this).

Although EDLIN is not as efficient and comprehensive as some full screen editors, there are some advantages to using it over a word-processing program.

One is that EDLIN is free—it is built-in as part of MS-DOS. Another advantage is that some word-processing programs make subtle changes to the text files. These are not changes you can see—but internal changes usually involving modification of the way the file is stored. This can be a problem if you try to use a word-processed file with another program, want to share a file with someone who has a different editor, or attempt to display the file using the MS-DOS TYPE command. These word-processed changes can cause the display of the file's contents to resemble some as yet undiscovered language.

You ASCII Me and I ASCII You

To eliminate some of these problems, most text files are stored in a format known as an *ASCII file*. ASCII (American Standard Code for Information Interchange) is a specific code scheme which the computer uses to recognize letters, numbers, and the punctuation marks that make up a text file. ASCII files contain their text information in exactly the same format as it is entered. When displayed, ASCII files make perfect sense.

ASCII is the most widely used format for computer files and it is used by most personal computers. One big advantage of entering your data in ASCII code is that these files can be used by many types of programs. This increases the flexibility of your data files. EDLIN enters and stores files in ASCII code.

In addition to the letters, numbers, and punctuation marks that you enter into an ASCII file, there are a few characters that ASCII itself adds to help format the text in a way it can easily understand.

ASCII indicates the "end of each line" by inserting two characters, the carriage return and the line feed. These characters carry the message "stop this line and move down to the next line."

At the conclusion of each file, ASCII inserts a marker to indicate the "end of the file." This character is "Ctrl Z", often written with a caret (^) to indicate the control key (^Z = Ctrl Z). These ASCII punctuation characters are hidden from view; you do not see them when you display or print out ASCII text files.

What's in an ASCII File?

An ASCII file contains:
the text of a file
end of line characters
end of file character (^Z)

Use ASCII format for:
text files
source code for programs
batch processing files

ASCII text files are used in three main areas of data entry—text files, written source code for programs (source code means the way the programs look as you type them in), and batch processing files (batch processing is covered in Chapter 8). When you create your files with EDLIN, you are joining this ASCII club and making your files as useful as possible. But now, onto the nitty gritty of actually using EDLIN.

As Easy As...

Because EDLIN is a line editor, it identifies all information in terms of *line numbers*. You do not enter these line numbers as you enter text, they are automatically supplied by EDLIN. Line numbers are only reference points within the file, they are not part of the *data* contained in the file. For example:

```
1: This is the first line of text,
2: You do not enter the line number as part of the
   file,
3: The numbers are supplied automatically by EDLIN,
```

Lines within the file are numbered in sequence. When new lines are inserted, or lines are deleted, EDLIN renumbers the lines automatically. But it doesn't *show* you the renumbering until you ask to see the file again. This is a bit confusing at first.

Suppose you want to add a new line at the beginning of an existing file (you'll learn how to do this in just a minute). This is a file about computer history and right now, the first line reads:

```
In the beginning there was ENIAC,,,
```

When you create or display this file using EDLIN, the first line appears like this:

```
1: In the beginning there was ENIAC,,,
```

But you have decided to change your opening. Now you want the first line to read: "And on the eighth day She created computers." This is how your file would appear after the insertion:

```
1: And on the eighth day She created computers,
2: In the beginning there was ENIAC,,,
```

Thereafter, if you wanted to modify "In the beginning there was EN-IAC...", you would need to refer to it as line number 2.

Short and to the Point

EDLIN receives its instructions from you in the form of commands. Commands are indicated by one letter abbreviations. Many commands also require that you indicate *which line or line numbers* are to be affected by the command. The format of EDLIN commands is simple. First you enter the beginning line number, then the ending line number (when line numbers are present they are separated by commas), and finally the single letter abbreviation indicating the command. Here are some examples of EDLIN commands:

Format of EDLIN Commands	
1D	Delete line 1
1,9L	List the file starting with line 1 and ending with line 9
4I	Insert a new line before line 4
E	End the editing session

Each EDLIN command is discussed in detail in this chapter.

Current Events

Inside EDLIN, the *current line* (the line you are working on or the last line you modified) is indicated by an asterisk after the line number and preceding the text on that line. If line 2 is your current line, it appears like this:

```
2:*In the beginning there was ENIAC...
```

Using the current line as a marker can help you move through your file more quickly. For instance, to make modifications to your current line you do not need to enter the current line number. Instead you enter a period:

.D   Tells EDLIN to delete the current line.

You can use the current line in place of a starting line number as a "shortcut" to get to a new location. To do this, you indicate the new location relative to the current line using a plus or minus sign and a number:

+35   Refers to the line that is 35 lines after the current line.

-54   Refers to the line that is 54 lines before the current line.

Until you have become more familiar with EDLIN, you can use actual line numbers to get to the line you want. Later you might find using the current line useful for faster moving in a large file.

In addition to being a marker of the current line, EDLIN also uses the asterisk as a *command prompt*. When EDLIN is waiting for a command or for you to enter some information, the asterisk appears on the far left of the screen and is not associated with a line number. When the asterisk is located after a line number, it is indicating the current line.

Two Uses of Asterisk

2:*In the beginning there was ENIAC...   * indicates the current line.

*   * indicates waiting for input.

Okay, with this brief introduction to line numbers, commands, and current lines you are all warmed up to begin using EDLIN.

Getting into the Act

In earlier chapters you have learned the advantages of "doing it yourself." Each use of MS-DOS commands becomes easier when you participate in the learning. Up until now you have been learning the fundamentals and this book has encouraged you to take part. Because this book is based strongly on the "immersion" theory of learning, you are now going to take this participation one step further. Not only will you be learning through practice, you will be doing it in the guise of a series of "personae," each designed to demonstrate an important aspect of MS-DOS. No costumes or Academy-award performances are required, just use your imagination to star in these scenarios.

Your first role will not take you far from home. In this scene you are an overworked, underpaid, harried worker who is definitely in need of some time-saving organization. Sound familiar?

Every Friday you leave the office with fresh determination to accomplish all those chores that you have been putting off. Every Monday morning you wonder *"where did the week-end go?"* Well, all of this is about to change. As the owner of a new personal computer, you are about to *get organized*. In fact, that was one of the reasons you bought your computer in the first place. On this early Friday evening you begin by making a list. Here's how it looks:

CHORES

Jody's soccer game, 9:00
Chad's little league game, 12:00
go to grocery store
mow lawn
put up hammock
dog to vet
get dog flea collar!
tennis with Annie, 2:00

Open Sesame

To begin this play, you must get your computer set up and ready to "run." Take your system diskette (your write-protected backup version of your system diskette) and insert it in drive A. Using the DIR command, make sure this diskette contains the EDLIN.COM program:

```
A>dir edlin.com <ENTER>

    Volume in drive A has no label
    Directory of A:\

EDLIN      COM      4608   3-08-83   12:00P
          1 File(s)      31232 bytes free
```

Next take a formatted diskette with plenty of space available and put it in drive B.

As you contemplate creating your first file, you may find yourself in a quandary—what should you call this new creation? In the interest of time, let's call it "chores." With that decided, you're ready to begin. To create a file, EDLIN needs two facts, the name of the program and the name of the file.

Is the A prompt on the screen? The A drive should be your current drive. You are going to create this file on the diskette in drive B, so you must include the *drive indicator* (b:) in the command:

```
A>edlin b:chores <ENTER>
```

EDLIN responds promptly with the following:

```
New file
*
```

Well, so far so good. Yes, this is a new file. "*" is the *EDLIN prompt,* so that tells you the program is waiting for further instructions.

EDLIN returns this "new file" message after it searches the diskette on the indicated drive and *does not* find an existing file with the entered filename. In other words, since there is no "chores" file on the diskette in drive B, it assumes this is a new file.

EDLIN's Opening Speeches	
If EDLIN displays:	**It means:**
`New file`	There is no file by this name on the designated diskette.
`End of input file`	The file has been loaded into memory.
`*`	The file is too large to fit into memory; memory is filled up to 75% capacity. The remainder of the file is still on the diskette.

If you enter the name of an existing file, EDLIN reads this file into memory, and then returns a different message:

```
End of input file
```

There is only one instance in which you do not receive a message from EDLIN in response to entering a filename. This is when your file is so large that not all of it can fit into the computer's memory at one time. When this is the case, and it is rare that a beginner would have files this large, EDLIN reads in as much of the file as can fit, reserving 25% of the memory. EDLIN operates with this 25% "safety reserve" at all times. If this instance should occur, EDLIN will simply display the asterisk prompt (*) with no additional message. Later we will describe some commands for creating space within memory and moving data around when your file is very large.

EDLIN has given you the prompt "*" and is awaiting your command.

Putting Thoughts into Words

Now you are ready to type your list of chores into the file. You inform EDLIN that you want to begin entering text by typing in the letter "I". As in MS-DOS commands, you can use upper- or lowercase letters to enter commands.

I stands for insert. While you are not strictly inserting information (since no information currently exists in the file), this is the command that EDLIN uses to begin new files. As you might suspect, you also use the I command to insert information into existing files, but first things first:

```
*i <ENTER>
```

EDLIN accepts your instructions and presents you with the first line number. The entire screen now looks like this:

```
New file
*i
    1:*__
```

Begin to type in your list. The first line of your file is your title "Chores." You must indicate the end of every line with <ENTER>. Each time you press the <ENTER> key, EDLIN will automatically supply a new line number for the next entry.

```
    1:*Chores <ENTER>
    2:*
```

If you make typing mistakes, just use the <BACKSPACE> key to erase characters (*before* pressing <ENTER>) and type the entry again.

Entering Information into an EDLIN File

Text and commands may be in upper- or lowercase.

Use <ENTER> to indicate the end of each entry.

Command format: starting line number, ending line number, command.

Correct mistakes with <BACKSPACE> before pressing <ENTER>.

This is quite a list, but now that you're organized, think of how much more efficient you will be. When you have entered all the items, you will have nine lines of text. EDLIN will be waiting for line 10. The file looks like this:

```
 1:*Chores
 2:*Jody's soccer game, 9:00
 3:*Chad's little league game, 12:00
 4:*go to grocery store
 5:*mow lawn
 6:*put up hammock
 7:*dog to vet
 8:*get dog flea collar!
 9:*tennis with Annie, 2:00
10:*
```

After you have entered the last chore, you are ready to exit from the "insert" mode. To return to "command mode" (EDLIN is ready to receive commands), you use the ^C (<Ctrl> C) function. (IBM users use the <Ctrl> <Break> key combination.) Remember that you must hold down the <Ctrl> key while you press the letter key. Both keys are released together. Enter this <Ctrl> C combination now in response to the prompt for line 10:

```
10:*^C

*
```

The asterisk, which has been keeping track of the current line, returns to the prompt position at the far left. You are now back in "command" mode.

Final Curtain

There is one more step to take before leaving the EDLIN program completely. You must tell EDLIN that this is the end of the file. And, logically enough, you do that by using the E (END) command.

The E (End) Command

use: indicates the conclusion of an editing session

example: e

When you finish entering text in an EDLIN file, you must first exit the "insert" mode (using ^C) and then give the end of the file signal to EDLIN by entering the E command. End the "chores" file now:

```
*e <ENTER>
```

As soon as you enter this command, EDLIN returns control to the operating system (indicated by the A> prompt).

```
A>
```

In and out with EDLIN

These are the steps to take to go into EDLIN, and return again to MS-DOS at the completion of the EDLIN program.

A>	start out in operating system
edlin *filename*	call the EDLIN program
i	enter the "insert" mode
lines of text	enter the content of the file
^C	exit the "insert" mode
e	exit the EDLIN program
A>	returned to operating system

Well bravo! Your debut as an EDLIN operator gets rave reviews. To verify that your role was as successful as it seems, take a look at your completed "chores" file.

Fine, you'd love to, but you are looking at an A> prompt. Where is your EDLIN file? Why, stored safely away on the disk, of course. Use DIR to check for the presence of "chores". Remember you indicated that this file was to be on drive B when you entered the original filename. Don't forget to include the drive letter now that you are looking for the file:

```
A>dir b:chores <ENTER>
```

No surprise, there is your "chores" list on the directory.

```
    Volume in drive B has no label
    Directory of B:\

CHORES           175    12-17-84       8:50a
     1 File(s)      361472 bytes free
```

Going over Your Lines

There are two ways to check the *contents* of an EDLIN file. The first requires the use of the MS-DOS TYPE command discussed in full in Chapter 6. Here is a sneak preview of TYPE. Enter this command and watch what happens:

```
A>type b:chores <ENTER>

Chores
Jody's soccer game, 9:00
Chad's little league game, 12:00
go to grocery store
mow lawn
put up hammock
dog to vet
get dog flea collar!
tennis with Annie, 2:00
```

There is your file, exactly as you entered it. But notice one thing. There are no line numbers. That's because line numbers are not part of the data in EDLIN files, they are simply reference points to use when editing or creating EDLIN files.

The second way to see the contents of your file is to use the EDLIN L (List) command. More about this command a little later in this chapter. Right now you are going to learn about another way to lower the curtain on an editing session.

The Q (Quit) Command

use: ends an EDLIN editing session without saving any changes

example: q

In addition to the E command, there is another way to end an editing session using EDLIN—you can use the Q (Quit) command. Choose the Q command when you want to *stop editing,* but don't care about saving the new file or any changes you have made to an existing file. The Q command does not write your file back to the diskette, it simply cancels the current editing session.

You might want to stop a session because you find that you don't really want to make any changes, or because perhaps things have gotten very mixed up and you just want to throw this session away. This is the time for the Q command.

Don't confuse the E (End) and the Q (Quit) commands:

E is for END,
Save for the next day.
Q is for QUIT,
Toss this #%&* thing away.

EDLIN provides a safeguard to prevent the loss of changes that you really intended to keep. When you enter the Q command, EDLIN asks:

```
Abort edit (Y/N)?
```

This is your last chance. A "Y" response sends the information entered in this editing session into the nearest black hole. An "N" response lets you continue with the edit.

Revising the Script

Now that you have created a file, and seen it safely put away, it's time to learn how to make changes in an EDLIN file. Be sure your system diskette (containing the EDLIN.COM file) is in drive A and the diskette containing your "chores" file is in drive B. Now ask for the file:

```
A>edlin b:chores <ENTER>
```

Since the file named "chores" already exists, EDLIN responds with the appropriate message:

```
End of input file
*
```

The asterisk prompt indicates EDLIN is waiting in the command mode. It's ready to make any required modification. There is one problem though—where is the text of the file?

You must remember that EDLIN moves one step at a time. All you requested was access to the file. Now EDLIN is waiting to find out which part of the file you want to see. You have to issue a command to look at your file.

Looking at the First Draft

The L (List) Command

use: lists the contents of an EDLIN file

examples: L
            1,9L
            43L

The L command allows you to look at a file, or a section of a file, while the EDLIN program is in operation (TYPE lets you look at the contents from MS-

DOS). As with many EDLIN commands, LIST requires the use of line numbers so that EDLIN can find the correct location in the file. As discussed earlier, EDLIN commands follow this pattern: *starting line number, comma, ending line number, letter of the command* (some commands require additional information).

Following this pattern, enter the L command to display the "chores" file:

```
*1,9L <ENTER>

    1:*Chores
    2: Jody's soccer game, 9:00
    3: Chad's little league game, 12:00
    4: go to grocery store
    5: mow lawn
    6: put up hammock
    7: dog to vet
    8: get dog flea collar!
    9: tennis with Annie, 2:00
*
```

The command told EDLIN to list lines 1 through 9 of the file. If you enter the L command without any line numbers, EDLIN lists the 23 lines centered on the current line number. (The asterisk indicates that line 1 is the current line, which makes sense since you have just opened the file.) Displaying the section immediately surrounding the current line makes working with large files easier when you want to see an overview of the section you are editing. Since "chores" is so short, you could have entered L without a line number and the entire file would have been displayed. Longer files require that you limit your range of line numbers to 23, since this is the maximum number of lines that can be displayed at one time.

There are other ways to use the L command. The L command with one line number lists the 23 lines starting with that line number, no matter what the current line number is. For example, *43L would list from line 43 through line 65.

Getting the Right Line

Okay, as the week-end moves closer, it's time to get those chores in order. Glancing over your list, you detect a few minor conflicts. You decide that while you can most definitely go to the soccer game at 9:00 and, barring excessive overtimes, make the little league at 12:00, there is no way you can play tennis at 2:00 and get anything else done. So you make a quick call, *"Sorry Annie, how about a bit of twilight tennis?"* Since it is forecast to be in the high 90's tomorrow afternoon, Annie quickly agrees *"Tennis at 7:00."*

Now it's time to update your file. To edit a *specific* line within an EDLIN file, enter the line number in response to the asterisk prompt. This command has no letter of the alphabet, simply enter the single line number. Your tennis match is on line 9:

```
*9 <ENTER>
```

EDLIN immediately displays a copy of that line, in its current version. You are then offered a seemingly blank line, preceded by the *same line number.*

```
9:*tennis with Annie, 2:00
9:*
```

This new line will contain the edited version of the current line. To update your list, you want to change the time of this appointment to 7:00. For now, type in the line again, changing the time. (There are some nice shortcuts you can use in editing lines in EDLIN files. You will learn about these tricks in the section on special keys in Chapter 7.)

```
    9:*tennis with Annie, 7:00 <ENTER>
*
```

This is all that EDLIN shows you, it *doesn't* show you the correction *right now.* To see how changes affect the contents of an EDLIN file, you must use L to list the file again.

```
*1,9L <ENTER>

    1: Chores
    2: Jody's soccer game, 9:00
    3: Chad's little league game, 12:00
    4: go to grocery store
    5: mow lawn
    6: put up hammock
    7: dog to vet
    8: get dog flea collar!
    9:*tennis with Annie, 7:00
  *
```

Sure enough, tennis with Annie is now scheduled for 7:00.

If you don't want to make any changes in a line once you have called for it, press <Ctrl> C. The line remains unchanged and you are returned to the * prompt.

Adding New Parts

The I (Insert) Command

use: inserts new lines into an EDLIN file

examples: i
            4i
            #i

Of course, once you sat down and started thinking about it, you remembered another thing that you really wanted to do this week-end—go to the computer store and get that hot new game your son was telling you about. Well, let's add it to the list. To add new lines, use the I command, the same one you use to create a new file.

You have to give some additional information to EDLIN when you use the I command to insert new information into an existing file. You must tell EDLIN *where* to insert the new line. You indicate the line number *before* the line where you want to make the insertion.

Since your list shows you going out to the grocery store anyway, why not put the computer store right above the grocery store on our list. As with other EDLIN commands, you enter the line number first and then the command. You want to insert this new line before line 4:

```
*4i <ENTER>
```

The screen displays the line number and waits for the new line:

```
4:*
```

Now type in your addition:

```
4:*go to computer store <ENTER>
```

EDLIN will continue to supply you with new line numbers for insertions until you exit the "insert mode" using the ^C keys.

```
5:* ^C

*
```

Calling for a listing with the L command displays the changes:

```
*L <ENTER>

    1: Chores
    2: Jody's soccer game, 9:00
    3: Chad's little league game, 12:00
    4: go to computer store
    5:*go to grocery store
    6: mow lawn
    7: put up hammock
    8: dog to vet
    9: get dog flea collar!
   10: tennis with Annie, 7:00
  *
```

The new line has been assigned line number 4, and all the remaining items on the list have been moved down one line number. There are now a total of ten items on the list.

Sometimes you may want to add new information at the end of a file. This presents a problem because no line number currently exists that you can insert *before*. EDLIN solves this situation by providing the # symbol. Using # in conjunction with an editing command means "do this operation at the end of the current file in memory." If you had wanted to add the store trip to the end of the file, you would have entered this command:

```
*#i <ENTER>
```

In response to this command, EDLIN presents a line number that is one higher then the current total number of lines in the file:

```
11:*
```

You would then type in the new line or lines. EDLIN keeps supplying line numbers after every <ENTER>. But you don't want this item on your list twice (it's long enough as it is). So just press ^C to tell EDLIN you are finished with entering new information. Line 11 will remain blank and will not be included in the file. If you are skeptical, check your file using the L command. If the line did somehow sneak in there, the next command tells you how to get rid of it.

Eliminating Unneeded Characters

The D (Delete) Command

use: deletes lines from an EDLIN file

examples: 86d
            1,5d

Looking over your list, it seems like things are beginning to pile up. And after all, this is the week-end; you deserve some time off. Maybe you can get the kid next door to mow the lawn and put up the hammock. Then you can relax in the yard after your tennis game. You're in luck, the kid agrees to do those chores (for a fair price of course). That's two things you can eliminate from your list.

To delete lines in EDLIN, you enter a starting line number and an ending line number. In effect, these two line numbers form a *block* of the information you want to eliminate. This block concept is useful for performing several commands in EDLIN. A block can also be only one line, in which case the starting and ending line numbers are the same and need be entered only once.

First double-check the line numbers of the items you want to delete by displaying the file with the L command:

```
*L <ENTER>

    1: Chores
    2: Jody's soccer game, 9:00
    3: Chad's little league game, 12:00
    4: go to computer store
    5: go to grocery store
    6: mow lawn
    7: put up hammock
    8: dog to vet
```

```
 9: get dog flea collar!
10: tennis with Annie, 7:00
*
```

In the current version of the file (since you added the computer store), "mow lawn" and "put up hammock" are line numbers 6 and 7. To delete these lines, enter this command:

```
*6,7d <ENTER>
*
```

And they are vanished, to trouble your conscience no more. To check to see that they are really gone, use the L command:

```
*L <ENTER>
```

Here is your new revised listing:

```
1: Chores
2: Jody's soccer game, 9:00
3: Chad's little league game, 12:00
4: go to computer store
5: go to grocery store
6:*dog to vet
7: get dog flea collar!
8: tennis with Annie, 7:00
*
```

You'll notice in this new listing that your original items 6 and 7 are now deleted and the remaining items have been renumbered. You're doing pretty well, considering that you haven't left the house yet and you've already cut the entire list down to 8 chores.

Comparison of Insert and Delete			
Insert		**Delete**	
i	begin a new file	d	delete the current line
6i	insert a new line 6 line 6 becomes line 7	6d	delete line 6 line 7 becomes line 6
#i	add new lines at end	1,6d	delete lines 1 through 6 line 7 becomes line 1

The S (Search) Command

use: searches for a string in an EDLIN file

examples: 1,8sdog
            1,8?sdog

Often when you are using EDLIN, you want to find a specific place in a file by searching for a particular word or pattern of characters within the file. In computereze, a group of characters (whether or not they make up an English "word"), is called a *string*. You might, for instance, want to edit a section of a file dealing with the string "CHRISTMAS", or you may want to check that you changed all those "STRONG AND SONS" to "STRONG AND ASSOCIATES" in a letter. To do this you use the S command.

In addition to the string, which tells EDLIN *"what I should search for,"* the S command also needs to know *"where should I search for it."* You give EDLIN this information by indicating the starting and ending line numbers of the "block" to be searched.

Since you have made several modifications to your "chores" file, you want to make sure that the trip to the vet is still on the agenda. You want to search the entire file (lines 1 through 8) for the string "dog".

The S command follows this pattern: line number to begin the search, a comma, line number to end the search, the S command, and then the string to be searched for. Enter the S command to find your dog:

```
*1,8sdog <ENTER>
```

EDLIN begins searching at line 1 and reports the first match:

```
    6:*dog to vet
*
```

If you want to continue the search for other occurrences of "dog", enter the S command again:

```
*s <ENTER>
```

EDLIN displays the next match:

```
    7: get dog flea collar!
*
```

When you enter S without any new "string," EDLIN uses the last string it was told to search for.

There is one catch with the S command. It only finds *exact* string matches. If dog appeared in our file as Dog or even DOG or as part of another word, DOGMA, these instances would not be reported by EDLIN.

Each time you enter the S command, EDLIN continues searching for "string matches" until it reaches the last line number entered. If it does not find the string, it sends this message:

```
Not found
```

There is a variation to the S command which allows you the option to continue searching after each occurrence of the string without re-entering the S command. To do this "global" search, insert a ? in the initial S command. Try looking everywhere for your dog:

```
*1,8?sdog <ENTER>
```

Notice that the question mark is entered *before* the S command. Because you included a ? in the S command, EDLIN asks you if this is what you were looking for or if you want to continue searching:

```
    6: dog to vet
O.K.?
```

If you answer "N", EDLIN continues to make matches. A "Y" answer indicates this is where you want to be, and the search ends.

The R (Replace) Command

use: replaces a string in an EDLIN command with another string

examples: 1,8rdog^Zdog and cat
            1,8?rdog^Zdog and cat

The R command is related to the S command, in that it too goes through the file searching for the specified pattern. R, however, allows you to replace every instance of your pattern with new information.

As you are reading over your list you get a revelation. The cat needs a shot too and she certainly needs a flea collar. To put this information on your list you want to search through "chores" for "dog" and replace it with "dog and cat".

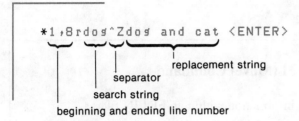

```
*1,8rdog^Zdog and cat <ENTER>
```
replacement string
separator
search string
beginning and ending line number

The beginning line number is followed by the ending line number. Then comes the R command preceding the string to be searched for. The R command requires one additional piece of information, *the replacement string*. A ^Z character separates the two strings. The R command automatically replaces every occurrence of the old string with the new string.

```
     6: dog and cat to vet
     7: get dog and cat flea collar!
*
```

As in the S command, you can use ? with the R command. This is useful if you are not certain you want to replace *every occurrence* of the string. When you include ? in the command, EDLIN asks if you want to make the replacement:

```
*1,8?rdog^Zdog and cat <ENTER>
     6:*dog and cat to vet
O.K.?
```

Use "Y" to approve the replacement and instruct EDLIN to continue with the search. It then displays the next occurrence of the string:

```
     7: get dog and cat flea collar!
O.K.?
```

If you answer "N" to this query, no replacement occurs in this line, but the search continues until the ending line number is reached.

These commands, Insert, Delete, Search, and Replace, are useful editing tools when you are dealing with small changes in just a few lines. But there are times when you will need to make changes involving large sections of a file. These require additional EDLIN commands.

Major Revisions

The M (Move) Command

use: moves blocks of information within an EDLIN file

example: 6,7,4m

You use the M command when you want to relocate a block of information within a file. Because you want to accomplish all your "car related" chores at one time, you decide to move the "animal items" right up there with the store items. It's much more efficient to have your list in neat chronological order.

The M command requires a beginning and an ending line number which define the block to be moved. You must also indicate the place you want the block *to be moved to*. Just as in the I command, you indicate the line number *before* which you want the items to appear. Since the vet is farther away than the computer store, and, after all, efficiency is the name of the game, you move lines 6 and 7 to *before* line 4.

```
*6,7,4m <ENTER>
*
```

Notice that in addition to the comma separating the beginning and ending line numbers, you must also put a comma between the ending line number and the line number indicating the new location.

Now you have modified your list a lot. Time to see what the newest version looks like:

```
*L <ENTER>

    1: Chores
    2: Jody's soccer game, 9:00
    3: Chad's little league game, 12:00
    4:*dog and cat to vet
    5: get dog and cat flea collar!
    6: go to computer store
```

```
    7: go to grocery store
    8: tennis with Annie, 7:00
  *
```

Looks like a full, but satisfying, day.

The C (Copy) Command

use: duplicates lines within an EDLIN file

example: 2,4,7c

Another useful way to move lines around inside an EDLIN file is with the C command. Just like the M command, the C command requires three line numbers, the starting and ending block line numbers, and the line number *before* which the copied lines should appear.

In our "chores" file, you don't really have a need to put duplicate lines elsewhere in the file, but for practice let's copy lines 2 through 4 and put them before line 7:

```
*2,4,7c <ENTER>
*
```

The resulting list looks like this:

```
*L <ENTER>

    1: Chores
    2: Jody's soccer game, 9:00
    3: Chad's little league game, 12:00
    4: dog and cat to vet
    5: get dog and cat flea collar!
    6: go to computer store
    7:*Jody's soccer game, 9:00
    8: Chad's little league game, 12:00
    9: dog and cat to vet
   10: go to grocery store
   11: tennis with Annie, 7:00
  *
```

The three copied lines appear twice in the list, in their original location as lines 2, 3, and 4 and as new lines 7, 8, and 9. But this makes no sense, so delete lines 7, 8, and 9:

```
*7,9d <ENTER>
*
```

All right, take a third curtain call. You have passed your opening night performance with nary a forgotten line or missed cue. The lucky character in this play can now take Sunday off, and you deserve a rest too.

The remaining EDLIN commands require two files or one very large file, so you won't actually perform these commands. Be sure and read through the description of these three commands so you will be familiar with their capabilities when you need to use them.

The T (Transfer) Command

use: moves lines from one EDLIN file to another

example: 8tb:schedule

T is yet another line-moving EDLIN command, but in this case it is from one file to another, not to different locations within a file.

Here is a hypothetical situation where you would use this command. You have another file on the diskette in drive B entitled "schedule". This contains a list of appointments that you want included in your "chores" file. You want to merge these two files.

You are going to add the contents of "schedule" to the "chores" file right before your tennis engagement, which is line number 8. The T command requires you to give EDLIN these pieces of information: the line *before* which you want the transfer made, the drive containing the diskette which holds the file, and the filename (with extension if necessary) of the file to be transferred. To merge these two files the T command looks like this:

```
*8tb:schedule
```

The contents of "schedule" would now appear in the "chores" file, located immediately before line 8.

The W (Write) Command

use: writes lines to a diskette from a file in memory

example: 2222w

As mentioned earlier, you may at some point be working with EDLIN files that are so large that they exceed the 75% memory capacity which EDLIN allocates for file size. In this case you will need to work with your file in parts.

You know that an entire file is not in memory, because EDLIN does not return the "End of input file" after you load a file. Instead only the asterisk appears.

To access the part of your file that is still on the diskette you must first clear out some space in memory. This is the function of the W command. To use W, enter the number of lines that are to be written back to the diskette followed by the command:

```
*2222w
```

In response, EDLIN writes the first 2222 lines back to the diskette. If you enter W without any line numbers, EDLIN writes back lines until memory is 25% full.

The A (Append) Command

use: writes lines from a diskette into memory

example: 2222a

After you have made room using the W command, you want to transfer the next section of your file into memory. The A command adds new text to the EDLIN file currently in memory. This command also uses the specified line number as a total count of lines to be moved. To add 2222 lines to the file enter this command:

```
*2222a
```

If you don't specify any line numbers here, EDLIN automatically fills memory up to its 75% working capacity.

It is unlikely that you will be using the W and A commands in the near future as they are required only when editing very large files.

Well, strike the set and call it a wrap. That's EDLIN, in it's entirety. Although a lot of information was presented in this chapter (and much of it may seem intimidating to you right now), don't worry. EDLIN is just like acting, after a while you have your stage directions down pat and you can just get on with the show. In this chapter you have learned what an editor is and how to use the MS-DOS EDLIN editor. In addition to creating a new file, you now know how to use all the EDLIN commands, E, Q, L, I, D, S, R, M, C, T, W, and A. If you can make a word out of that, go to the head of the class!

In the next chapter you are going to learn lots of fascinating facts about files and how to use MS-DOS commands to manage the files you create and edit with EDLIN.

6

Getting the Files in Shape

6 Getting the Files in Shape

Now you're ready to run the full mile and find out "everything you ever wanted to know about files." You've done your stretching exercises by learning the DIR and CLS commands. You've mentally prepared yourself by studying about diskettes and becoming acquainted with the FORMAT and DISKCOPY commands. And you've taken a practice lap by creating a file with EDLIN. You're ready for the MS-DOS marathon!

What Exactly Is a File?

The term "file" is not unknown to you. You've been working with files for a while now. You listed files with DIR, copied files with DISKCOPY, and created files with EDLIN. In this chapter you will learn about the intricacies of naming files and how to use MS-DOS to manage your files. First a quick summary.

A file is a group of related data, stored together in one location. File is not a term restricted to the high tech world of computers—you use files everyday in a variety of ways. When you stack all your phone bills in one pile, you're creating a file. When you add a memo to a project report at work, you're expanding a file. When you delete from your address book the names of people who moved away ten years ago, you're updating a file.

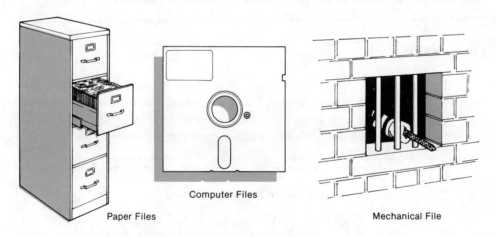

Paper Files   Computer Files   Mechanical File

Types of files.

Computer data files perform this same organization and storage function, but they happen to reside on diskettes. When DIR displays the contents of a diskette, it details the information about each file—its filename, its size in bytes (remember each byte represents one character in a file), and the time and date the file was created or last modified. To MS-DOS all data is part of one file or another.

Of course *file* is also a verb, as in filing your income tax or filing it away in the "to be done" drawer, or even "filing your way to freedom," but in this discussion, file is a noun and defines a collection of related data.

What's in a Name?

To create, store, and retrieve files, they must be named. Otherwise how would MS-DOS differentiate among the thousands of files it has to keep track of? And how would you know what was in each of those files? To alleviate confusion, MS-DOS has established a very simple rule.

The Golden Rule of Filenaming

Each file on a diskette must have a unique name!

The reasons for this rule are pretty obvious to anyone who has been blessed with a common name such as Mary or John, or Smith or Johnson. Someone calls out a name and you, along with five or six other people, questioningly point at yourself or hesitantly raise your hand. Well the same is true of your files. If more than one has the same name, MS-DOS is totally confused. You have to be very specific.

Here is another example of the necessity for unique names. Imagine a group of participants all milling around at the beginning of a track meet. If the announcer calls over the loud-speaker *"Racers to their marks, please,"* confusion reigns. Which racers for which race to which marks? This problem is solved by adding specific information that clarifies the instructions. *"Attention participants in the 400-yard dash: racer 2 report to lane 1, racer 4 report to lane 2, racer 6 report to lane 3, and racer 8 report to lane 4."* Adding specific identifications clears up ambiguities and assures that everyone is in the correct location.

Here's how this same confusion might happen within DOS. One of the commands you will learn about in this chapter is COPY. If you type in this command like this:

```
A>copy
```

MS-DOS contemplates a nervous breakdown. Copy what, from where, to where? You'll see how to enter this command with all the necessary information in just a second.

Official Rules and Regulations

When you assign each file a unique filename all these problems are laid to rest. Now both you and MS-DOS know exactly which file is to be created, modified, operated upon, or stored away. A filename must follow this pattern:

filename.extension

The *filename* can be from one to eight characters. An optional *extension*, not exceeding three characters, may be added to the name. When you give a filename an extension, use a period to separate the extension from the filename itself.

Filenames must follow one additional rule. They must be made up of *valid characters*. MS-DOS makes this pretty simple for us:

Valid Characters for Filenames

letters of the alphabet
numbers one through zero
special characters: $ # & @ ! % ( ) __ '

The exact list of special characters may vary depending on your computer type and the version of MS-DOS on your machine.

In general, these symbols may not be used in filenames:

Invalid Characters for Filenames

. (period, except to delineate an extension)   < (less than)
: (colon)   > (greater than)
- (hyphen)   \ (backslash)
/ (slash)   ¦ (vertical bar)
? (question mark)   * (asterisk)

These symbols have special meanings in MS-DOS and are misinterpreted if included within a filename.

There are also some special groups of characters that MS-DOS reserves for its own use. One group is the names of the MS-DOS commands and program files. You can't use such already existing filenames. Another group consists of *device names*. These are abbreviations that MS-DOS uses to refer to specific pieces of computer equipment.

If you use these combinations of characters in filenames, MS-DOS gets confused. Again, this list may vary from system to system. To really be sure about filename limitations, check your computer's user's guide.

Reserved Filenames and Device Names

ASSIGN	DATE	GRAPHICS	RD
BASIC	DEBUG	LINK	RMDIR
BASICA	DEL	MKDIR	SET
BREAK	DIR	MODE	SORT
CD	DISKCOMP	MORE	TIME
CHDIR	DISKCOPY	PATH	TREE
CHKDSK	EDLIN	PRINT	TYPE
CLS	ERASE	PROMPT	VER
COMMAND	EXE2BIN	RECOVER	VERIFY
COMP	FDISK	RENAME	VOL
COPY	FIND	REN	
CTTY	FORMAT	RESTORE	
AUX:	CON:	LPT3:	
COM1:	LPT1:	NUL:	
COM2:	LPT2:	PRN	

Seems like a pretty formidable list, huh? Well, believe it or not, by the time you finish reading this book you will know, and even be intimately acquainted with, at least 50% of these terms.

Except for these special cases, you can name your files almost anything. Here are some sample filenames:

    bills
    scores
    games
    letters

Just for convenience and to make typing them in easier, this book always shows filenames in lowercase letters. When you are using filenames in commands, you can enter them in either upper- or lowercase. When filenames are included in the text, they are enclosed in quotation marks (" "). For example: the "bills" file is …

A FILE BY ANY OTHER NAME

DAN DISK AND HIS DISKETTES

Avoiding Hyperextension

A three character extension in any filename is optional. Extensions are useful for clarifying or categorizing the contents of a file. For example, you have a file named "letters". Now, if you put all your letters into this one file, not only would it be very large, it would also be extremely difficult to use. Each time you wanted to look at a specific letter, you would have to search through the entire file. By subdividing this file into three smaller files with identifying extensions, you can save yourself a lot of time and trouble.

letters.bus   these are your business letters
letters.sue   these letters are of a more personal nature
letters.tax   legal correspondence concerning tax shelters

At first glance it would seem that these three files violate the sacred uniqueness rule for filenames. All of the files are named "letters"! But the extension, as a part of the filename, can be the differentiating factor. Sometimes it is even desirable to use similar filenames to group related files together. However, be prudent in doing so because too many similar filenames can cause you confusion.

While you can use any valid character in an extension, there is a loose sort of convention that has grown up among software designers to give certain types of files certain extensions. A few extensions are mandatory since they tell MS-DOS what to do with a file. For example, .BAS refers to a file that is written in BASIC source code. All BASIC files must have this extension. MS-DOS recognizes files with a .BAT extension as "batch files" (batch files are discussed in Chapter 8). Here are some of the most frequently used filename extensions:

.BAK   a backup copy of a text file

.BAS   a BASIC source code file

.BAT   a batch processing file

.COM   an executable program in memory-image format

.DAT   a general data file

.EXE   an executable program in relocation format

.TXT   a text file from a word processor

Don't worry if you don't understand these explanations. The only reason these extensions are mentioned at all is so you won't be alarmed if some strange extension shows up on one of your directory listings.

Probably the most important rule of naming files is to assign a name that makes sense to you. Although you can use many special symbols in filenames, what good is a file when you can't remember what's inside it?

Pop Quiz on Filenames

What's wrong with these filenames?

(Cover up the answers on the right-hand side of the page)

ZZZ#9HUH.YUK	This is a legal filename, but what's in it?
MYOWN/.TEXT	Two things are wrong here: / is an illegal character and there are too many characters in the extension.
FASTNOTES	A filename can have only eight characters.
COPY.BAS	Copy is a reserved filename.
DING.BAT	This is a perfectly valid filename, and I'm sure you'd remember what you put in it!

Set Specific Goals

The name of a file is made up of the filename (up to eight characters) and the optional extension (up to three characters). But when you use a filename in a command, MS-DOS must have one more piece of information—which drive contains the diskette that holds the file? You direct MS-DOS to the correct drive by including the letter of the drive (the drive indicator a: or b:) in the filename. You were introduced to this concept is Chapter 4 when you learned about the "current" drive and source and target diskettes.

Here's a quick review on drive indicators:

`A>a:games`	The drive indicator is optional because A is the current drive (as shown by the A prompt).
`A>games`	Produces the same results as the above command.
`A>b:games`	The drive indicator is mandatory because the file is not on the diskette in the current drive.
`B>a:games`	The same situation in reverse.
`A>format b:`	Drive indicator is mandatory for MS-DOS to perform the operation on the correct diskette.
`A>diskcopy a: b:`	Whenever you are transferring data from one diskette to another, it is a good idea to include both drive indicators.

Because you are going to use the COPY command later in this chapter, learning to use drive indicators takes on added significance. These three elements of a filename—the name itself, the optional extension, and the drive indicator—make up a *file specification.*

File Specification

drive indicator: + filename + .extension (optional)

And that's all you really need to know about naming files. This is one area where you can let your imagination run free, just remember a few special rules.

The Filename Pyramid

give each file a unique name
make filename easy to remember
include a drive indicator if necessary
no more than eight letters in a filename
no more than three characters in an extension
don't use invalid characters or reserved names
separate the filename from the extension with a period

Now that you've conquered filenaming, it's time to expand your routine a bit. Breathe deeply and jump into the command workout.

Commands, Inside and Out

Just as "file" was familiar to you from earlier chapters, so is the term "commands." You've been issuing commands since your first DIR experience. But now you are going to expand on that knowledge.

Command is another word that is not restricted to computer use. Any of you who have been in the Army or have suffered through dog-obedience courses with lovable Rover know about commands. Commands are simply clear and comprehensible instructions.

Commands in MS-DOS are instructions to the computer. As mentioned earlier, MS-DOS, while true and loyal, is rather stupid. It can only understand instructions when they follow a preordained pattern. The commands that you give MS-DOS must be very specific. Fortunately for users, MS-DOS commands make sense in English too. It's pretty simple now that you have used them a few times to remember that DIR stands for DIRectory, and CLS stands for CLear the Screen, while FORMAT and DISKCOPY are self-explanatory. You'll find the commands in this chapter just as clear and concise.

Internal and External Commands

There are some commands that are resident in your computer's RAM (transient) memory whenever you are operating under MS-DOS control, that is, whenever you are responding to the MS-DOS prompt (A> or B>). These commands are called *internal* because they are inside the machine's memory, ready for use whenever you are operating in MS-DOS. The following shows the "typical" MS-DOS internal commands.

Internal Commands	
COPY	makes copies of files
DATE	sets or displays the date
DIR	displays a list of files
ERASE (DEL)	eliminates a disk file
RENAME	changes a file's name
TIME	sets or displays the time
TYPE	displays the contents of a file

The internal commands in your version of MS-DOS may include other commands. Check your user's guide for the internal commands associated with your system.

The important thing to remember about internal commands is that you can use them any time after you have booted your system, without reinserting your system diskette. For instance, you might be running a program off the diskette in drive A, let's say a word-processing program. You have finished with the file, which is on the diskette in drive A, and you want to copy it to drive B. After exiting the word-processing program, you return to the MS-DOS system prompt. Your word-processing program is on Diskette 1, now in drive A. The file you want to copy is also on Diskette 1. Diskette 2 is in drive B. It contains text files and is the target diskette for your newly completed file.

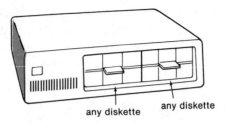

Boot system with MS-DOS diskette.
Internal commands are always available.

Using an internal command.

Because COPY is an *internal* command, you can use it without removing your word-processing diskette from drive A. The command is in memory, available for use no matter which diskettes are in the drives. Use caution, however; there is more to copying files than this. See the section on the COPY command before you copy anything.

Most MS-DOS commands do not make their home inside RAM memory. This means they are not available when you are "in" MS-DOS. These "external" commands must be loaded from the operating system diskette when you need them. To use these commands, you must have a system diskette in drive A.

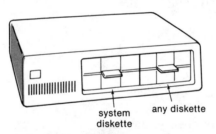

Boot system with MS-DOS diskette.
Must have system diskette in drive A
for external commands.

Using an external command.

When you enter a command, MS-DOS first checks to see if the command is internal. If the command is not found, MS-DOS goes out to the system diskette to find and load the command. If it is not on the diskette, or you don't have a system diskette in the drive, MS-DOS sends you a nasty error message such as:

```
Bad command or file name
```

FORMAT is an example of an external command. In the hypothetical example above (word-processing diskette in drive A, and data diskette in drive B), you may occasionally find yourself in a bit of a pickle. You want to transfer the file on Diskette 1 to a new diskette, Diskette 3, but first you need to FORMAT a diskette to receive the data.

Since FORMAT is an external command you must have a system diskette in a drive to make use of this command. (That is why you should have several formatted diskettes handy at all times.) To execute the FORMAT command, you must first remove your word-processing diskette and insert the system diskette. Only now are you ready to use the FORMAT command. (Of course, you better also remove the data diskette from drive B and insert a new blank diskette before entering the FORMAT command, or else you can say goodbye to the data currently on the diskette in drive B.)

Before you begin studying specific commands in detail, here are some helpful hints for entering all MS-DOS commands:

- Wait until you see the MS-DOS prompt (A> or B>) before entering a command. The prompt means DOS is up and waiting.

- When a command requires a filename to operate, be sure you include all of the necessary parts of the file specification (drive indicator, filename, and extension).

- Use a blank space to separate the different parts of a command.

  `format b:`   Leave a space between command and drive indicator.

  `copy olddata b:`   Leave spaces between command, filename, and drive indicator.

- You can enter commands in either upper- or lowercase.

- When commands don't work, check your typing. Is the command correct, did you leave the appropriate spaces, did you spell the filename correctly? Are you trying to use an external command without inserting the system diskette?

- End each command with the <ENTER> key.

This chapter covers four MS-DOS commands: COPY, TYPE, ERASE, and RENAME. They are all internal commands. But before you start copying, typing, erasing (especially erasing), and renaming files, you need a file to use with these commands. So let's put your EDLIN skills to work and create a new file.

Put your backup system diskette in drive A. Be sure it contains a copy of the EDLIN.COM program. The file you are creating will also be located on this system diskette.

The Great American Novel

Time to take on a new identity. In this chapter you are playing the role of a writer just embarking on a literary career. You are using your new personal computer to write your first work.

Your book text will be contained in a file called "novel". Using EDLIN, enter the text of this file. The first line of text is the title of this work, "EVEN MONEY":

```
A>edlin novel <ENTER>
New file
*i <ENTER>
        1:*EVEN MONEY <ENTER>
```

As EDLIN returns new line numbers, enter the remainder of the text. You're only going to get through the opening paragraph in this session.

```
2:*There was a 50/50 chance the world would end today. <ENTER>
3:*It was down to Just the three of us now. <ENTER>
4:*The "Stranger" kept watching the darkening sky. <ENTER>
5:*Finally he saw the signal. <ENTER>
6:*Tossing the quarter in the air, he laughed  "Call it"...<ENTER>
7:*
```

Use ^C to exit the "insert" mode.

```
7:^C
```

Now give EDLIN the end of file command:

```
*e <ENTER>
```

The system prompt tells you that MS-DOS is now back in control:

```
A>
```

If you want to, you can use DIR to verify that the file is on the diskette.

```
A>dir novel <ENTER>

 Volume in drive A has no label
 Directory of A:\

NOVEL              242 12-17-84    10:11a
         1 File(s)       30720 bytes free
```

Are you anxious to see your work in print? Well let's use a new MS-DOS command to see the contents of this file. You had a preview of this command in Chapter 5.

Reviewing What You Wrote

The TYPE Command

use: displays the contents of a file

example: type novel

TYPE is a very straightforward command. Used in conjunction with a file-name, it displays the contents of the file. The text of the file must be in ASCII format or you'll have a tough time deciphering it. If you missed it earlier, ASCII file format is discussed in detail at the beginning of Chapter 5. Since EDLIN creates files in ASCII code you will have no trouble reading your "novel":

```
A>type novel <ENTER>
```

The file contents appear (without line numbers):

```
EVEN MONEY
There was a 50/50 chance the world would end today.
It was down to just the three of us now.
The "Stranger" kept watching the darkening sky.
Finally he saw the signal.
Tossing the quarter in the air, he laughed "Call it"...
```

Not bad for a beginner.

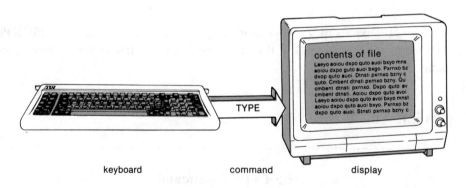

The TYPE command.

By including a drive indicator in the TYPE command, you can view files on other diskettes. Suppose you had created "novel" on the diskette in drive B. Then this is how you would ask to see the file:

```
A>type b:novel <ENTER>
```

Since you don't currently have the file on the diskette in B, this command will not work. But how do you go about making a backup of this copy to put on another diskette?

Where Is the Carbon Paper?

In today's world of information proliferation, rarely do you make just an original of anything. From term papers to tax forms, it's always smart to keep a copy. When the documents are on paper, you type multiple copies or more likely run down to the friendly copy machine.

Copies are useful for many reasons. They are handy if two or more people are referring to the same document. They allow you to share information that might not otherwise be available to someone. They provide a record of interaction between two companies or communication between two people. But by far the most persuasive argument for copies is that they provide "insurance" in case something should happen to the original. (This was discussed in some detail in Chapter 4.)

All of these reasons for making copies hold true for your computer files too. It is just as easy to copy a computer file as it is to copy a paper file, but you don't need any extra copying equipment. All you need is another diskette. How important are copies? Let's pick up on the saga of "EVEN MONEY".

Much as you would like it, you can't earn a living as an unpublished author. So your writing times are squeezed between the demands of the office and the need for sleep. Naturally, this time is precious to you. Late one evening, you start to work on some changes that your agent has suggested. After hours of work, you have incorporated the revisions into the text. But the very next day your agent phones and says *Scratch those changes, there may be a question of libel involved.*

Unfortunately, while you were editing the work, you entered and exited the EDLIN program several times, so even the EDLIN backup file no longer contains your original version. You do have a printout of the first few chapters, but that means entering lots of text again. MORAL OF ACT 1: MAKE A BACKUP OF YOUR ORIGINAL FILE (ON A SEPARATE DISKETTE) BEFORE YOU MAKE ANY SIGNIFICANT CHANGES.

Here's another short lesson on copying. Now you finally have your book back in order. You have been talking to a friend in Chicago about the possibility of turning this book into a screenplay. He is anxious to see the latest revision so, since you are going on vacation for a few days, you give him your diskette. Wouldn't you know it, while he is sorting through his diskettes he spills a cup of coffee. Your diskette was on the top of the pile. MORAL OF ACT 2: MAKE A COPY OF ALL FILES BEFORE THEY LEAVE YOUR POSSESSION.

I'm sure you are beginning to get the picture. The thing that is helpful to remember about diskette files, as opposed to paper files, is that unless you make one, there is no copy of anything in the file. You can't hunt through the waste-paper basket for the piece of information you deleted. But you can find it on a copy. Here are some reasons why you should make copies:

- for insurance

- in case you need a copy of an earlier version of the files

- to reorganize files

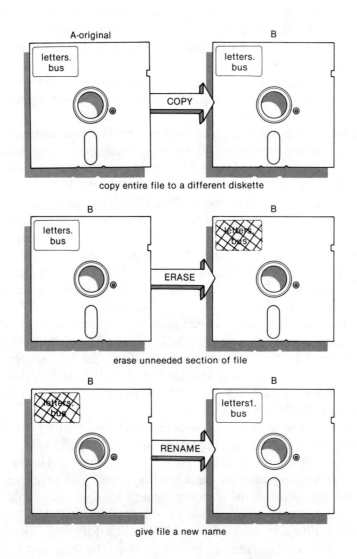

copy entire file to a different diskette

erase unneeded section of file

give file a new name

There are other, less drastic reasons to make copies. You might also copy files when you want to put them in new groups on a diskette or use parts of a file to reorganize its contents.

Earlier in this chapter you saw the advantage of grouping files using extensions:

letters.bus
letters.sue
letters.tax

Suppose the "letters.bus" file has become to large to be efficient. Here's how you would use a copy to solve that problem. Of course, you already have an updated backup of this file.

First, you make a copy of the entire "letters.bus" file. You want to make a new file that contains only the letters from the "Live Now, Die Later" company. By deleting all the other correspondence in your newly copied file you are left with only the relevant letters. You then give this file a new name using RENAME (a command discussed later in this chapter). Your results are one file "letters1.bus" which holds only a part of your original file "letter.bus".

In most cases, you will be copying from one diskette to another. This means you have to tell MS-DOS where to find the original and where to put the copy.

May the Source Be with You

You were introduced to the concept of *source* and *target* diskettes when you used the DISKCOPY command. They are equally important in the use of the command you are about to execute, the COPY command, and deserve a brief review here.

The source diskette contains the original file. The target diskette is the destination of the copied file. With two drives, the source is usually the diskette in drive A and the target is the diskette in drive B. MS-DOS reminds you to keep track of your source and target:

```
Insert source diskette in Drive A
Insert target diskette in Drive B
```

The source and target diskettes are indicated by drive specifiers (a: and b:).

If you have a single drive system, refer back to the discussion of DISKCOPY (in Chapter 4) to review how MS-DOS "pretends" you have two drives.

With this theoretical discussion of why and when to make copies behind you, revert to your novelist's role as you learn to use the COPY command.

Being Redundant

The COPY Command

use: makes copies of a file or a group of files

examples: copy a:novel b:
              copy a:novel b:bestsell
              copy novel bestsell

The COPY command is very versatile. One use of this command that you will make very frequently is to copy a file from one diskette to another, keeping the same name. (This is our old friend the backup.) Let's try this now. You will need your system diskette containing the created "novel" file and a *formatted* blank diskette to perform these copying exercises.

You want to make an "insurance" copy of your first edition of "EVEN MONEY". Take the diskette containing "novel" (in this case, your system diskette) and put it in drive A. This is your source diskette. It is just a coincidence that "novel" is on your system diskette. Since COPY is an internal command, it is not necessary to have the system diskette in a drive when you are executing this command. Put the diskette that will contain the copy in drive B. This is your target diskette.

The A> prompt shows you that drive A is your current drive. It is not necessary to include the drive indicator a: when referring to a file on this diskette in this drive. Just to keep things clear, however, it's easier to include the drive indicator in these copy commands. As you become more at ease with MS-DOS, you will probably not include the drive indicator when it is unnecessary.

Okay, now copy "novel" to the target diskette:

```
A>copy a:novel b: <ENTER>
```

With this command you tell MS-DOS to copy the file "novel" now on the diskette in drive A to the disk in drive B. The name of the copied file will also be "novel".

Here is how MS-DOS responds to this command:

```
1 File(s) copied
```

Short and simple but to the point. This message says *"fine;"* your request has been honored. This message is a very convenient part of MS-DOS because it lets you know several things at once. It tells you that the specified file was found on the indicated diskette, that there is no problem with the target diskette, and that the copying procedure is completed. If anything had gone wrong, such as an incorrect diskette inserted in A or an unformatted diskette in B, you would have received an error message.

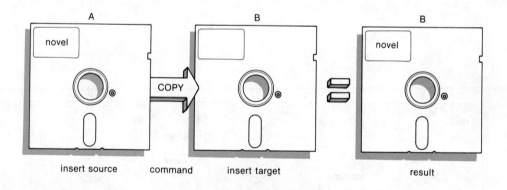

Copy to a different diskette.

This seems a little too simple. As a nervous writer, you want to be sure the copy is on the diskette in B. Relieve your skepticism by requesting verification with the DIR command:

```
A>dir b: <ENTER>
```

MS-DOS responds:

```
Volume in drive B has no label
Directory of B:\

NOVEL              242     12-17-84        10:11a
         1 File(s)        361472 bytes free
```

You don't have to use the same name when you copy a file. Suppose you want to copy the file and try changing sections of it. You want both a copy of the original and a copy to fool around with. You can copy the file and give it a new name. To do this include a new filename in the COPY command. Try copying your file, but change the name:

```
A>copy a:novel b:bestsell <ENTER>
```

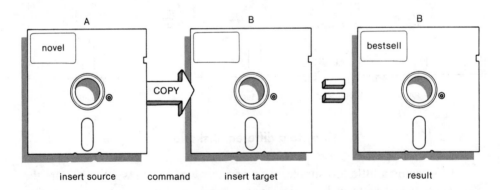

Copy to a different diskette, changing name.

Again comes your confirmation:

```
1 File(s) copied
```

If you have done both of the above exercises, you now have two files copied on the target diskette. One is called "novel" and the other is "bestsell". BOTH FILES CONTAIN EXACTLY THE SAME INFORMATION. To make sure both copies are on the diskette, use the DIR command:

```
A>dir b: <ENTER>

    Volume in drive B has no label
    Directory of B:\

NOVEL          242     12-17-84    10:11a
BESTSELL       242     12-17-84    10:11a
       2 File(s)     360448 bytes free
```

You can also have two copies of a file on the same diskette. But to copy a file to the same diskette, you have to give the file a new name because NO TWO FILES ON THE SAME DISKETTE CAN HAVE THE SAME NAME. Let's make a duplicate copy of "novel" on the diskette in drive A. In this case, the diskette in drive A is both our source and target diskette. This time try leaving out the drive indicators:

```
A>copy novel bestsell <ENTER>
          1 File(s) copied
```

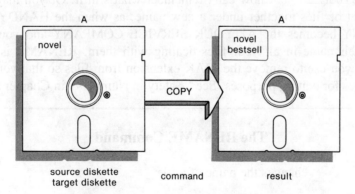

Copy to same diskette, changing name.

You now have two copies of the file on the same diskette. Only the names are different; the contents are the same.

MS-DOS will not let you copy a file to a diskette if that diskette already contains a file with an identical filename. This handy reminder comes in the form of an error message:

```
File cannot be copied onto itself
         0 File(s) copied
```

If you want to be sure that all your files are, in fact, duplicate copies of the same diskette, you can check their contents using the TYPE command:

```
A>type novel <ENTER>
A>type bestsell <ENTER>
A>type b:novel <ENTER>
A>type b:bestsell <ENTER>
```

The results of all these commands are the same because you have not altered the contents, just the filenames. The next command also allows you to change the name of a file.

A Rose by Any Other Name

There are several reasons why you might want to rename a file. It could be that you have files with very similar names and there is a danger of confusing them. Or you may, in a flight of fancy, have given your file the very esoteric name "ZST8$E__", but now can't remember what's in it. Or you may want to group a set of files together under a new name, as when the HANDYDANDY COMPANY becomes the AT YOUR SERVICE COMPANY and you need to change their name in all your files dealing with them. RENAME is also the command you use to remove the .BAK extension from files so that you can use backup files for editing purposes. See "Safety in Numbers" in Chapter 5.

The RENAME Command	
use:	changes the name of a file
example:	ren novel opus1
abbreviation:	ren

As an aspiring writer, you realize that there is another book inside you, dying to get out. The filename "novel" is now too limiting. You want to know *which* novel. So you decide to give your file the more specific name "opus1". Using the RENAME command, change the filename. You can enter this command with its entire name "RENAME" or you can use the abbreviation "REN". You must include the old and new name. To RENAME the file on the current drive you don't need to include drive indicators:

```
A>ren novel opus1 <ENTER>
```

This is a silent job by MS-DOS. It simply returns you to the A> prompt after renaming the file. To verify the name change you must use DIR:

```
A>dir <ENTER>
```

This gives you a listing of the entire diskette. Notice that the listing no longer contains "novel" but does contain "opus1".

You can also make sure that the change has occurred by using DIR with the new filename:

```
A>dir opus1 <ENTER>
```

MS-DOS confirms that the filename has been changed:

```
Volume in drive A has no label
Directory of A:\

OPUS1            242     12-17-84     10:11a
        1 File(s)        30208 bytes free
```

If you want to be absolutely sure that "novel" no longer exists, you can ask for a directory of that file:

```
A>dir novel <ENTER>
```

Because no file by that name is on the diskette, MS-DOS answers:

```
File not found
```

As with the other commands, you can RENAME a file on a drive other than the current drive by including a drive indicator. Now, RENAME the file "novel" that is on the diskette in the B drive by including the drive indicator in the command. Enter this command:

```
A>ren b:novel opus1 <ENTER>
```

"Novel" is no more. Again you will be returned to the system prompt. You still have two copies of the file on each diskette, but they are named "opus1" and "bestsell". A listing of the files on the diskette in B confirms this change:

```
A>dir b: <ENTER>

    Volume in drive B has no label
    Directory of B:\
```

```
OPUS1               242    12-17-84   10:11a
BESTSELL            242    12-17-84   10:11a
        2 File(s)       360448 bytes free
```

You may be confused as to how this command is different from using the COPY command with a new filename. Both change the name of the file.

COPY Versus RENAME

A>copy novel bestsell   creates a duplicate file with a new name

A>ren novel opus1   changes the name of the existing file

Wiped Out

Files seem to have the reproductive capacity of rabbits. Every time you think you have it under control, files seem to multiply at an alarming rate. Many of the files you use, such as program files, will serve you well for many years. Other files quickly become outdated or irrelevant. Even the worst packrat cannot save every file forever. Sooner or later you will want to do some housekeeping and clean up your files. You eliminate *unneeded* files with the ERASE command.

The ERASE Command

use: deletes files from a diskette

examples: erase bestsell

               del b:bestsell

NOTE: The DEL (Delete) command is identical to the ERASE command.

There is one thing to keep in mind when you are using the ERASE command: YOU CANNOT GET BACK FILES ONCE THEY HAVE BEEN ERASED. Before using this command, make sure that the intended victim is a duplicate or useless file. Also, enter the filename with care; if your files have similar names, a simple typing error can cause you great grief.

At this point, you have duplicated copies of your file on both diskettes. You want to do a little tidying up, so you are going to erase one of the files on each diskette. You decide to stick with the name "opus1" because it most clearly defines the file for you. Before you do any erasing, it's a good idea to make sure exactly which files are on a diskette. If you have a directory in front of you, you're less likely to enter a filename by error and find out too late that you made a mistake. A directory also confirms that the file you want to delete actually resides on the diskette.

With all of the copying and renaming that you have done on this file, you may be confused as to which names are still valid filenames. Get a directory of each diskette:

```
A>dir <ENTER>

    Volume in drive A has no label
    Directory of A:\

    COMMAND  COM    17664   3-08-83   12:00P
    ANSI     SYS     1664   3-08-83   12:00P
    FORMAT   COM     6016   3-08-83   12:00P
    CHKDSK   COM     6400   3-08-83   12:00P
    SYS      COM     1408   3-08-83   12:00P
    DISKCOPY COM     2444   3-08-83   12:00P
    DISKCOMP COM     2074   3-08-83   12:00P
    COMP     COM     2523   3-08-83   12:00P
    EDLIN    COM     4608   3-08-83   12:00P
    MODE     COM     3139   3-08-83   12:00P
    FDISK    COM     6177   3-08-83   12:00P
    BACKUP   COM     3687   3-08-83   12:00P
    RESTORE  COM     4003   3-08-83   12:00P
    PRINT    COM     4608   3-08-83   12:00P
    RECOVER  COM     2304   3-08-83   12:00P
    ASSIGN   COM      896   3-08-83   12:00P
    TREE     COM     1513   3-08-83   12:00P
    GRAPHICS COM      789   3-08-83   12:00P
    SORT     EXE     1280   3-08-83   12:00P
    FIND     EXE     5888   3-08-83   12:00P
    MORE     COM      384   3-08-83   12:00P
    BASIC    COM    16256   3-08-83   12:00P
    BASICA   COM    25984   3-08-83   12:00P
    OPUS1            242   12-17-84   10:11a
    BESTSELL         242   12-17-84   10:11a
            25 File(s)      30208 bytes free
```

Now take a look at the other diskette:

```
A>dir b: <ENTER>
    Volume in drive B has no label
    Directory of B:\

OPUS1              242       12-17-84      10:11a
BESTSELL           242       12-17-84      10:11a
          2 File(s)       360448 bytes free
```

First eliminate the "bestsell" file from the diskette in drive A:

```
A>erase bestsell <ENTER>
```

You don't get any response from MS-DOS when you use the ERASE command. To make sure the file is gone, use the DIR command:

```
A>dir bestsell <ENTER>
```

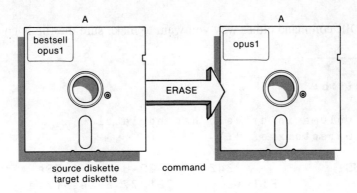

The ERASE command.

If everything has gone according to the script you get this message:

```
File not found
```

Don't panic! Are you worried that you have eliminated all traces of your book? Just ask for it by name:

```
A>dir opus1 <ENTER>

    Volume in drive A has no label
    Directory of A:\

OPUS1            242     12-17-84    10:11a
        1 File(s)        361472 bytes free
```

Perform the same procedure on the diskette in drive B:

```
A>erase b:bestsell <ENTER>
```

Use the DIR command either way you want to make sure the file is gone:

```
A>dir b: <ENTER>

    Volume in drive B has no label
    Directory of B:\

OPUS1            242      9-29-84     1:29p
            1 File(s)        361477 bytes free
```

Great! Everything is in tip-top shape. You have two copies of your book, one on the diskette in drive A and the backup on the diskette in drive B. Now you can get on with writing the *History of Civilization*.

Now you're right back where you started, two copies of the file, one on each diskette. This concludes your performance as the up-and-coming literary sensation of the 80s!

If you still feel a bit confused, it is worth your time to create, copy, type, rename, and erase some more files. These commands are really the "bread and butter" of your everyday work with MS-DOS. COPY especially is essential since you will be making frequent backups of your files. It may also surprise you how often you use TYPE to see the contents of a file. RENAME and ERASE are commands that become increasingly useful as you accumulate more and more files and want to clarify and keep clean your various directories.

This chapter has set a new pace for your conquest of MS-DOS. First you discovered files and learned the ins and outs of filenaming. You were then introduced to MS-DOS commands in general and the difference in the use of internal and external commands. In the guise of a struggling writer, you used EDLIN to create a file. Using this file you put MS-DOS to work by using the TYPE, COPY, RENAME, and ERASE commands. At the conclusion of this chapter, you are well on your way to effective file management using MS-DOS.

7

Shifting into High Gear

7 Shifting into High Gear

You can cast off your acting cloak for a while. This chapter is going to refine your computing skills so you'll be ready to use your computer to tackle even loftier roles in the future. In the last two chapters you have been working with files, creating them with EDLIN and managing them with the basic MS-DOS commands.

This chapter teaches you how to use your keyboard more effectively by presenting some special keys and key combinations that make file creation and editing easier. In addition, it expands on your knowledge of commands by showing you how to use *switches* with the DIR and FORMAT commands. Finally, three new commands are discussed: SYS, CHKDSK, and MODE.

Let Your Fingers Lead the Way

Through your experience with MS-DOS you have already become acquainted with some of the special keys on your computer keyboard. By this time you are probably becoming familiar with the location of the standard alphabet, number, and punctuation keys.

The first two special keys are already in your repertoire. They are included here as a brief review.

The <ENTER> Key

use: indicates the end of an entry

The <BACKSPACE> Key

use: moves the cursor to the left along a line

     <BACKSPACE> erases characters as it moves

You wouldn't be this far along unless you had already mastered the <ENTER> key. This important key must be pressed to give the go ahead signal to MS-DOS. This key may look like this < ↵ > on your keyboard.

And unless you are perfect, you've probably had a lot of experience with the <BACKSPACE> key as well. This key is an easy way to erase characters to correct mistakes. You will learn some additional mistake-correcting procedures later in this chapter. This key may be represented as a left arrow <←> on your keyboard.

141

<ENTER> key
end of entry

<BACKSPACE> key
erase characters

The <ENTER> and <BACKSPACE> keys.

Now we are going to introduce some other keys that make using MS-DOS and EDLIN more convenient. One word of caution, your keyboard *may not* contain some or any of these keys. But by reading through the entire section on editing characters, you will find out how to use your keyboard to the best advantage.

Most of these keys are only operational when you are using MS-DOS and/or EDLIN, although there are exceptions. They usually are inoperative or perform different functions in other programs. After a little experience in a variety of computing applications, you will learn the "quirks" of each key and its uses.

The <Caps Lock> Key

use: enters all alphabetic keys in uppercase
<Caps Lock> does not affect number or punctuation keys

when <Caps Lock> is in effect, pressing <SHIFT> causes all alphabet keys to be entered in lowercase

---

You have used the <SHIFT> key to enter uppercase letters, but you may not know that there is another key which also lets you type in uppercase. This is the <Caps Lock> key. When <Caps Lock> is not in use, all letter and number keys are normally entered in lowercase. When you turn on <Caps Lock> mode by depressing this key, all letters are entered in uppercase. <Caps Lock> affects only the *letter keys* on your keyboard. <SHIFT> is still required to enter the punctuation symbols found above the number keys and on the upper section of other keys. <Caps Lock> mode stays in effect until you depress the key again.

Here is one rather unique result of using the <Caps Lock> key that may surprise you. When you are in the <Caps Lock> mode, pressing the <SHIFT> key causes all letters to be entered in lowercase. Try using <Caps Lock> to enter some information, just to get the general idea.

In Normal Mode (<Caps Lock> off)

Pressing <M> results in m
Pressing <SHIFT> <M> results in M
Pressing <SHIFT> <2> results in @

In Caps Lock Mode (<Caps Lock> on)

Pressing <M> results in M
Pressing <SHIFT> <M> results in m
Pressing <SHIFT> <2> results in @

<Caps Lock>

<Caps Lock> key.

The <Esc> Key

use: cancels the current line. <Esc> must be pressed before the <ENTER> key

---

Suppose you discover that you have made a mistake on an entry as you just finish typing in the entire line. Of course, the mistake is way back at the front of the line. You just don't feel like sitting there using <BACKSPACE> to erase the whole thing. There is a way to cancel an entire line.

To eliminate a line you use the <Esc> (Escape) key. <Esc> puts a back-slash (\) on your command line to indicate that the command is canceled. It then moves the cursor down one line so you can enter a new command. When you cancel a line with <Esc> it is not received by the computer. Try this now. Imagine that you are looking for a file on the directory called fishing.123. As you enter the extension you realize that you have made a mistake:

```
A>dir wishing.123 <Esc>
```

After you press <Esc> the screen looks like this:

```
A>dir wishing.123\     The <Esc> key cancels this command and moves
                       you down to the next line.
__                     Cursor appears waiting for a new command.
```

You could now enter the correct information and continue with your work. Additional editing commands will be explained in "The Editing Express" later in this chapter.

The <Esc> and <PrtSc> keys.

The <PrtSc> Key

use: <SHIFT> <PrtSc> prints everything currently displayed on the entire screen

<Ctrl> <PrtSc> echoes each line to the screen as it is entered

---

Often, when you are entering or editing commands or text, you may want to have a printed copy of what is being displayed on the screen. To do this, you use the <PrtSc> (Print Screen) key. If you do not have this key, there is also a way for you to print out your display. See the <Ctrl> P description on page 155.

To print out everything that is currently displayed on your screen, first be sure your printer is turned on and ready. When you print out the contents of a display it is known as "dumping the screen." To perform this dump, hold down one of the <SHIFT> keys and press <PrtSc>.

You can also make a printed copy of everything you enter on the screen, *at the same time as you enter each line*. This is called "echoing" the screen to the printer. To echo each line as it is entered, hold down the <Ctrl> key and press the <PrtSc> key. All typed-in entries are echoed to the printer until you press <Ctrl> <PrtSc> again.

The <Num Lock> Key

use: switches the numeric keypad between numbers and cursor control

<Ctrl> <Num Lock> stops the screen from scrolling

The keys on the numeric keypad on your machine have a dual purpose. They may be used to enter numbers as input or to control the movement of the cursor.

These keys will have a set of arrows and terms such as "Home", "End", "PgUp" (page up), and "PgDn" (page down). The <Num Lock> key controls which function these keys perform.

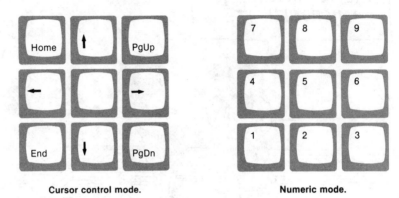

Cursor control mode.   Numeric mode.

The numeric keypad.

Normally, <Num Lock> is in the cursor control mode. This means that pressing the keys moves the cursor up, down, left, right, or to a certain location on the screen or in a file. These cursor control keys are not normally used in MS-DOS operation but they are used in many application programs.

Pressing <Num Lock> while it is in this cursor control mode shifts the keyboard to the numeric mode. Now, when you press these keys, the numbers are entered as input. However, when using MS-DOS you will probably use the number keys across the top of the keyboard for numeric input.

When you look at a piece of information that is more than 23 lines long, the screen will scroll. As new information appears on the bottom of the screen the entries at the top disappear. Remember what happened the first time you used DIR to look at the contents of your system diskette? To stop the screen from scrolling, use the <Ctrl> <Num Lock> key combination. To "unfreeze" the screen, press the <SPACEBAR> key or <Ctrl> <Break>.

If you do not have <Num Lock> on your keyboard, you can stop the screen from scrolling too. See the <Ctrl> S description on page 155.

The Editing Express

Whether you are writing the great American novel, figuring how you can make the most of your new tax shelter, or creating your first BASIC program, most of your interactions with the computer take place via the keyboard. And, unless you are a typing champion, you will frequently make mistakes while entering your information.

Now, as Mr. Rogers tells us, *"Everyone makes mistakes, oh yes they do..."* Most computer programs provide some help for you in correcting these mistakes.

A word processor, for example, allows for certain keys that help you move forward and backward in a line or around in a file to change information, or even provide internal spelling checks. BASIC, the programming language your computer most likely uses, has a built-in editor to help make error correction easier. MS-DOS also provides some special keys to speed up the editing process when you are entering commands or using the EDLIN program.

Any line that you type into the computer is stored in a special place in the computer's memory. This location is called the *input buffer*. As soon as you press <ENTER>, the last line you typed is retained in the input buffer. The line currently stored in the input buffer is called a *template*. By recalling this template, you can use it as a pattern and make minor changes within a line using just a few keystrokes.

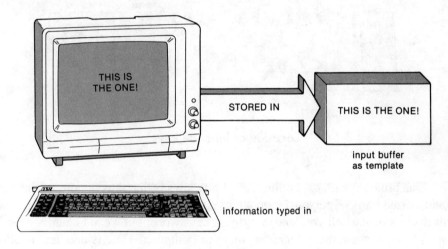

Template in the input buffer.

How can this template help you? Well, most of the commands and other information you enter into MS-DOS consist of very short lines. Commands, after all, are rarely more than 4 letters and filenames will never exceed 12 characters. MS-DOS editing keys are designed to make correcting mistakes in these short lines easier and faster.

The Functions at the Junctions

Some of the editing keys are already familiar to you. You know about using <Esc> to cancel the line you are typing and you have used <BACKSPACE> to erase characters on a line. The other editing operations require the use of *function keys*, those strange keys with F1, F2, etc. enscribed on them, or a combination of two keys.

Location of function keys.

One problem with explaining the editing keys is that they are one of the least standardized parts of personal computer systems. That means, unfortunately, that this discussion can tell you *how* the editing keys work, but it can't identify exactly *which* keys perform these functions on your computer. Here is another situation where you must check your user's guide to find out the specifics for your machine.

If you have numerous function keys on your keyboard, you are probably in luck. Most often these function keys provide the editing operations with one keystroke.

The reference chart on page 154 lists the most frequently used key for each function. If the keys your computer uses are different from those listed, write down the keys you use in the blank box before the description of each operation.

But how do you actually use the editing keys? Let's look at a hypothetical situation. You have a file in which the last line reads like this:

```
This is the final line. <ENTER>
```

Now you want to make some editing changes in that line.

The <F3> (Copy All) Function

use: copies the entire template

Once you have pressed the <ENTER> key, this line becomes the template in your input buffer. But then you decide you want to add more information at the end of the line. First you need to recall the line from the template. To retrieve the entire line you use the *copy all* function.

```
This is the final line.    You press <F3> (copy all).
```

MS-DOS returns the template:

```
This is the final line.    To add more information, first erase the
                           period using the <BACKSPACE> key,
This is the final line     then type in the new text:

This is the final line of this program. <ENTER>
```

Now "This is the final line of this program" is your template.

The <F1> (Copy One Character) Function

use: copies one character at a time from the template

You can use the editing keys to copy part of a line. There are several ways to do this. The simplest is to *copy one character* at a time.

```
This is the final line of this program.    Press <F1>.
T                                          If you press
This                                       <F1> four
                                           times.
```

The <F2> (Copy Up To) Function

use: copies the characters in the template up to the first occurrence of the specified character

---

There is a quicker way to copy part of the template, however. You can use the *copy up to* function, <F2>. "Copy up to" means retrieve all of the template up to a specified character. The specified character is not included in the new template.

```
This is the final line of this program.    Press <F2>
This is the                                and then "f".
```

"Copy up to" copies up to the first occurrence of the indicated letter. Suppose the line in the template was:

```
This is often the final line of this program.   Press
                                                <F2>
                                                and
                                                then
This is o                                       "f".
```

The characters in the template are copied up to the first occurrence of "f" in the word "often". To copy up to the word "final" you would enter <F2> and "f" once more.

```
This is o            You press <F2> and then "f".
This is often the
```

The <Del> (Skip Over One Character) Function

use: skips over the next character in the template

You can also use the editing keys to skip over part of the template. You use the <Del> key to *skip over one character.*

```
This is the final line of this program,
```
You press <Del> and then <F3> to copy the remaining characters.

```
his is the final line of this program,
```
If you press <Del> and <F3> again:

```
is is the final line of this program,
```

The <F4> (Skip Up To) Function

use: to skip over characters in the template up to the first occurrence of the specified character

Just as you can copy up to, you can also "skip up to." To do this you use the <F4> key and indicate the character you want to skip up to. The specified character is not included in the template.

```
This is the final line of this program,
```
You press <F4> and then "n". Press <F3> to copy the remaining characters.

```
nal line of this program,
```

Just as "copy up to" copies up to the first occurrence of the character, "skip up to" skips all characters up to the first occurrence of the letter given.

```
This is the final line of this program,    You press
                                           <F4> and then
                                           "l". Press
                                           <F3> to copy
                                           the remaining
                                           characters.

l line of this program,
```

You may have been intending to skip up to the word "line" but the "l" in final is encountered first. Pressing <F4> and "l" again brings you up to the desired location in the template.

The <Ins> (Insert a New Character) Function

use: inserts new characters into the existing template

You can also insert new information into the middle of a template. To do this you use the <Ins> key. This may seem tricky. See if you can follow this example.

```
This is the final line of this program,    You press
                                           <F2> and then
                                           "o".
This is the final line                     Press <Ins>,
                                           type "and end",
                                           and then press
                                           <F3>.
This is the final line and end of this program,
```

Did you get all that? If not, just take another look. First you copied the template up to the first occurrence of the letter "o" (in the word "of"). Then you pressed the <Ins> key to indicate that you wanted to add new characters. The characters added are "and end ". <F3> then copies all the remaining characters in the template resulting in the new line. Once you get used to them, these function keys can really cut your editing time.

The <F5> (Create a New Template) Function

use: makes the most recently entered line the new template

The <F5> editing key makes your current line the new template. In the previous example, pressing <F5> after you had finished editing the line, but before you had pressed <ENTER>, would make "This is the final line and end of this program" the template. Note that while this line is now the template, it has not been sent to the computer. If the new line was a command, it would not be executed by the computer. Suppose the most recent line read:

COPY a: b: You do not press <ENTER> at the end of the line, but do press <F5>. Then you press <F3>.

COPY a: b: This is the new template but the command has not been sent to the computer.

The <Esc> (Escape) Function

use: cancels a line (the template is not affected)

Surprise! You already know how to use this function. This is just a reminder that <Esc> is a function as well as a key. When you use <Esc> to cancel a line, the template is not changed (that is, it is not canceled and left blank). The last line entered is still the current template. The backslash on the line indicates that it has been canceled.

```
This is the final line      You press <Esc>.

This is the final line \
```

The line entered *just before* this one would still be the template.

Using editing keys takes a bit of getting used to and you may be a little confused until you get the hang of it. But these keys can be very useful when you are entering duplicate or repetitive commands or when you want to correct mistakes without typing in the entire line again. Experiment with these keys and see if they are helpful to you.

The following is a reference chart of the editing functions and the *probable* keys used to perform each function.

Editing Functions and Keys			
Your Key	**Key**	**Function**	**Explanation**
	<Esc>	cancel	cancel the last line
	<BACK-SPACE> <←>	back up	erase the last character
	<F3>	copy all	copy the entire template
	<F1>	copy one	copy one character
	<F2>	copy up to	copy up to a specified character (character is not included in the copied template)
	<Del>	skip one	skip one character in template
	<F4>	skip up to	skip up to the specified character (specified character not included in the template)
	<Ins>	enter new characters	insert new information in the middle of the template
	<F5>	new template	make this line the new template (if a command, not executed until <ENTER> is pressed)

Exercising Control

Throughout this book you have been gradually introduced to the <Ctrl> key in its various guises. You used <Ctrl> <Alt> <Del> to perform a warm boot and you used <Ctrl> S to stop the screen from scrolling.

Some computer keyboards use specific keys to perform specific actions such as <PrtSc> and <Num Lock> described previously. But if your machine does not have these special keys you can use <Ctrl> in conjunction with another key to perform these actions. Even if you do have these special keys, you can use the <Ctrl> combinations too because these keys are standard on all computers using

MS-DOS. These control functions operate not only in MS-DOS but also in a wide variety of other programs. They are presented in a chart for quick reference.

Control Functions and Keys	
Keys	**Explanation**
\<Ctrl\> \<Alt\> \<Del\>	reboots the MS-DOS system
\<Ctrl\> C	cancels the current line (like the \<Esc\> key) or cancels the currently running program
\<Ctrl\> H	moves the cursor to the left and erases the last character, just like the \<BACKSPACE\> or \<←\> key
\<Ctrl\> P	echoes the display to the printer, line by line
\<Ctrl\> N	turns off the echoing function
\<Ctrl\> S	stops the scrolling on the screen; to resume scrolling press any key
\<Ctrl\> Z	end of file marker

Dealing with a Full Deck

Special keys, function keys, and control key combinations help you use MS-DOS and EDLIN with less wasted motion. Not surprisingly, filenames also have a few shortcuts that can increase your standing as an efficiency expert.

You probably haven't thought of your experience in computing as resembling a card game, although you have taken a few chances. But now you are going to learn to use that old favorite of traveling gamblers, *wildcards*.

Like their playing card antecedents, wildcards can stand for something else or a lot of something elses. When used in filenames, wildcards replace one or more specific characters in the filename or extension.

As you know, each file's name must be unique, but many of your filenames probably have a lot in common. Wildcards allow you to perform an action on a group of similarly named files, using only one command. The wildcard replaces one or more characters in the filename. Wildcards are especially useful when you are using the DIR, COPY, ERASE, and RENAME commands because in these situations you are frequently referring to *groups of files*.

The wildcard symbols (sometimes called *global characters*) are the question mark (?) and the asterisk (*).

The question mark is used to match *one character in one specific character position* in a filename or extension. For example, if you had all your monthly salary records on one diskette, the files might look like this:

```
JA-MAR.SUM
JANSAL.
FEBSAL.
MARSAL.
MARTOT.
JA-JUN.SUM
```

You want a directory of all the files that concern monthly salaries. You could look at the whole directory or use DIR to check on the presence of each individual salary file. But you can get this information much quicker by entering this command:

```
A>dir ???sal <ENTER>
```

The following directory would appear:

```
Volume in drive A has no label
Directory of A:\

JANSAL          128       8-1-84          12:24P
FEBSAL          128       8-1-84          12:24P
MARSAL          128       8-1-84          12:24P
        3 File(s)      294912 bytes free
```

This command tells MS-DOS: *look through the directory of the diskette in drive A and list all files which end in "sal"*. Any characters may be used in the first three positions. The use of the question mark in the first three positions means that each of these files fulfills the qualifications of the command. This is the key to the question mark wildcard; any character can occupy the position indicated by the ?, but the rest of the name must be *exactly the same*. If you had entered:

```
A>dir mar????? <ENTER>
```

then these files would be listed:

```
Volume in drive A has no label
Directory of A\:

MARSAL          128       8-1-84          12:24P
MARTOT          128       8-1-84          12:24P
        2 File(s)      294912 bytes free
```

In response to this command, MS-DOS looks for files that have "mar" in the first three positions and any characters in the last five positions.

When you include the ? wildcard as the last character in a filename or extension, you must account for all eight characters in the filename proper or all three characters in the extension.

The asterisk wildcard is just like using a lot of question marks. When you include an "*" in a filename specification, *any character can occupy that position or any of the remaining positions* in the filename or extension. An asterisk pretends that there are as many question marks in the filename as there are positions.

Asterisks do not include the extension of a filename unless you specify this with another asterisk after the period. Then it will accept any extension. If, for our above files, you entered this command:

```
A>dir ja*.* <ENTER>
```

MS-DOS would list the following files:

```
Volume in drive A is has no label
Directory of A:\

JA-MAR     SUM       128    8-1-84     12:24P
JANSAL               128    8-1-84     12:24P
JA/JUN     SUM       128    8-1-84     12:24P
            3 File(s)     294912 bytes free
```

Here MS-DOS is looking for any files that contain JA in the first two positions. Any characters can occupy the remaining positions in the filename. Since you also included an asterisk in the extension, the filename can contain any extension.

And for a completely wild filename:

```
*.*
```

As you have probably guessed, this means all files!

Wildcards can be useful because of their power, but they can also be dangerous. When you want to copy all of the files on a diskette (copy *.*) or list an entire directory (dir *.*), they can make your task easier.

Beware of the use of wildcards with the ERASE command. As you probably guessed, ERASE *.* would mean goodbye to all the files on your diskette. MS-DOS is looking out for your best interests, though. When you use *.* with the ERASE command, MS-DOS gives you a chance to back out. When you enter:

```
A>erase *.* <ENTER>
```

You get this message:

```
Are you sure (Y/N)?
```

Enter "Y" if you are really sure or "N" if you have any doubts about what you're doing.

This concludes your lesson in "Special MS-DOS Shortcuts." The keys, functions, and tools described in this chapter move you up one notch on the climb through the "discovery mountains" of MS-DOS. Now you're going to go back and visit some familiar spots along the way, but with a few new twists and turns.

Some Old Friends Revisited

As you become better acquainted with MS-DOS, you not only are able to use it more easily, but you come to appreciate some of its finer points. Up to this point, you have been using commands in their simplest form. These are valid uses of commands. But there are some options to commands that can make them even more useful.

Commands can contain *switches*. As the name implies, switches can turn on and off certain operations within a command. When you add a switch to a command you indicate it with a slash (/) and a letter. Switches always follow the command and any drive indicators.

The DIR Command (The Second Time Around)

use: displays a directory of the specified diskette or lists the specific attributes of a single file

switches: /w display the directory in several columns across the screen (only the filenames are displayed)
            /p pauses when the directory fills one screen

examples: dir/w
            dir/p

You are familiar with your first MS-DOS friend, the DIR command. You know this command lists the files on a directory, displaying their names, extensions, sizes, and the time and date they were last accessed. If the directory contains more files than will fit on one screen, the display scrolls until it reaches the end of the listing.

There are two optional switches you can include in the DIR command that alter how the directory is displayed, /w and /p. The /w switch lists the files in columns across the screen.

Assume that the diskette listing you want to see is in drive A and this is your current drive. You enter the command like this:

```
A>dir/w <ENTER>
```

If this diskette is a typical system diskette the listing look like this:

```
    Volume in drive A has no label
    Directory of A:\
COMMAND  COM ANSI     SYS FORMAT   COM CHKDSK COM SYS     COM
DISKCOPY COM DISKCOMP COM COMP     COM EDLIN  COM MODE    COM
FDISK    COM BACKUP   COM RESTORE  COM PRINT  COM RECOVER COM
ASSIGN   COM TREE     COM GRAPHICS COM SORT   EXE FIND    EXE
MORE     COM BASIC    COM BASICA   COM
        23 File(s) 31232 bytes free
```

This horizontal layout of the directory can be useful when the diskette holds a lot of files and you want to see only their names. Note that this directory does

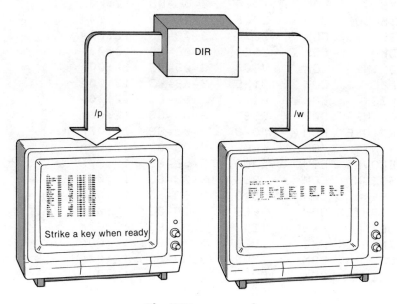

The DIR command.

not give you any information about file size or the date or time the file was last accessed.

The other switch used with the DIR command is /p. The /p switch operates like an automatic scroll control. It stops the display of a directory when the screen is filled. This switch is useful when you want to look at the listing of a large directory. You can study the display, and then indicate when you are ready to proceed. Again, the switch follows the command:

```
A>dir/p <ENTER>
```

This is how the result of this command appears on the screen:

```
Volume in drive A has no label
Directory of A:\

COMMAND   COM    17664    3-08-83    12:00P
ANSI      SYS     1664    3-08-83    12:00P
FORMAT    COM     6016    3-08-83    12:00P
CHKDSK    COM     6400    3-08-83    12:00P
SYS       COM     1408    3-08-83    12:00P
DISKCOPY  COM     2444    3-08-83    12:00P
DISKCOMP  COM     2074    3-08-83    12:00P
COMP      COM     2523    3-08-83    12:00P
EDLIN     COM     4608    3-08-83    12:00P
MODE      COM     3139    3-08-83    12:00P
FDISK     COM     6177    3-08-83    12:00P
BACKUP    COM     3687    3-08-83    12:00P
RESTORE   COM     4003    3-08-83    12:00P
PRINT     COM     4608    3-08-83    12:00P
RECOVER   COM     2304    3-08-83    12:00P
ASSIGN    COM      896    3-08-83    12:00P
TREE      COM     1513    3-08-83    12:00P
GRAPHICS  COM      789    3-08-83    12:00P
SORT      EXE     1280    3-08-83    12:00P
FIND      EXE     5888    3-08-83    12:00P
MORE      COM      384    3-08-83    12:00P
BASIC     COM    16256    3-08-83    12:00P
BASICA    COM    25984    3-08-83    12:00P
```

When the entire screen is filled, MS-DOS gives this message:

```
Strike a key when ready . . .
```

You press any key and the directory continues:

```
23 File(s) 31232 bytes free
```

While DIR/p takes up more space than DIR/w on your screen, it has the advantage of allowing information on all files to be displayed in a fashion that's convenient to read. It also provides complete information on each file.

Now, you're probably getting the idea of switches. Another command you are familiar with also has optional switches.

The FORMAT Command (New and Improved Version)

use: readies a diskette to receive data

switches: /v gives the diskette a volume label
            /s puts the operating system on the diskette during the for-
                matting procedure

examples: format b:/v
            format b:/s

As you know, FORMAT sets up your diskette to receive information. Up to this point we have not discussed a very important capability of FORMAT—the ability to put a name on a diskette.

How many times have you looked at the results of a DIR command and wondered *"Why doesn't the volume in drive A have a label?"* You keep getting this same message over and over but can't do anything about it. Well, the time has come.

The *volume name* (which simply means the name of the diskette) can be helpful to you in identifying the contents of a diskette. To put a volume name or volume label (as MS-DOS refers to it) on a disk, you use the /v switch.

Let's put a volume label on a diskette we're going to use for examples in Chapter 10. Put your system diskette in drive A and a new, unformatted diskette in drive B. Be sure it is empty because the FORMAT command will erase any existing information on a diskette.

Okay, now begin the procedure by entering the FORMAT command and including the /v switch:

```
A>format b:/v <ENTER>
Insert new diskette for drive B:
and strike any key when ready
```

Check, you've already put in your new diskette, so FORMAT away:

```
Formatting...Format complete
```

So far everything seems exactly normal. But now MS-DOS inserts a new message:

```
Volume label (11 characters, ENTER for none)?
```

Here is your chance to individualize your diskette. You can name the diskette anything you want up to 11 characters. Name your diskette "wine cellar". An intriguing title. Are you peeking at Chapter 10 right now? If you had decided against including a volume label, you would just press <ENTER>. Type in the volume label now:

```
Volume label (11 characters, ENTER for none)?wine cellar <ENTER>
```

The formatting then continues as usual:

```
    362496 bytes total disk space
    362496 bytes available on disk

Format another (Y/N)?n
```

The diskette is now ready to receive data. How do you know the volume label of a diskette? Enter the DIR command and you'll find out:

```
A>dir b: <ENTER>

    Volume in drive B is WINE CELLAR
    Directory of B:\
```

The contents of the diskette would then be listed. Since you don't have any files on this diskette yet, you will see this message:

```
File not found
```

The /s switch on the FORMAT command allows you to put a copy of the operating system on a diskette. This can be a timesaver because *it allows you to boot the system from any diskette that has been formatted this way.*

For example, you may write a program that you know you will use quite often. This program requires you to input information from a data diskette. Well, if you have the system on your program diskette, you can just insert it in drive

A, insert the data diskette in drive B, turn on the machine, and away you go. No more inserting the system diskette in drive A, then removing this diskette to put in your program diskette, and then beginning to run the program.

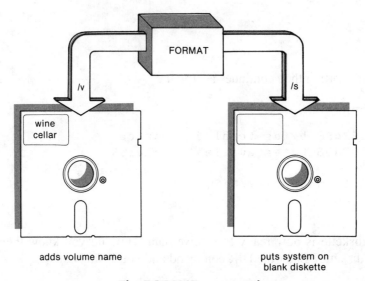

adds volume name   puts system on
                                    blank diskette

The FORMAT command.

When you include the /s switch in the FORMAT command to set up a system diskette, it transfers three files to the new diskette. Two of these files are *hidden*. It doesn't mean DOS can't find them. It means you won't see them listed among the files on a diskette when using the DIR command. The CHKDSK command, coming up soon, *will* tell you if a diskette contains any hidden files. These files cannot be accessed by you, that way you can't change them or do anything to make the system act crazy. The third file transferred by the /s switch is COMMAND.COM. This file does appear as part of a diskette's contents when you use DIR to look at the diskette. All three of these files make up the *system*.

Putting the system on the diskette does take up some space. Not every diskette needs to have the system on it. However, if you think you are likely to be booting from a diskette or you know you will need the internal commands handy when you are using the diskette, put the system on it. You can take the COMMAND.COM file off (using ERASE) if you find you need more space on the diskette.

Important Notice!

Hear ye! Hear ye! You must include the /s switch at the time you format the diskette to put the system on a blank diskette.

To format the diskette in drive B and make this diskette a system diskette, enter the command and the switch:

```
A>format b:/s <ENTER>
```

MS-DOS follows the usual steps in the formatting sequence:

```
Insert new diskette for drive B:
and strike any key when ready

Formatting...Format complete
```

Here's the new twist, an added message:

```
System transferred
```

The space occupied by the system is included in the message at the completion of the formatting operation:

```
    362496 bytes total disk space
     40960 bytes used by system
    321536 bytes available on disk

Format another (Y/N)?n
```

And that's all there is to it! You now have a self-booting diskette ready for your data or programs.

You can put a volume label and the system on the same diskette. Simply enter both switches at the time you FORMAT the diskette:

```
A>format b:/v/s <ENTER>
```

On some computers the order of the switches does not matter. Others require the /s to come last. You can never go wrong by indicating the /v first and the /s second.

You will see the "system transferred" message and be asked for a "volume label" during the formatting procedure.

Remember, the /s switch is only for transferring the system on to a new, blank diskette. Since you will quickly find how convenient it is to have the system on a diskette, your next logical question is *"How can I put the system on diskettes that already contain information?"* Read on.

Making New Acquaintances

The SYS Command

use: transfers the hidden files of MS-DOS to a disk

example: sys b:

The SYS command performs the same function as the /s switch in the FORMAT command. That is, it transfers the operating system onto a designated diskette. Since the use of FORMAT erases all previous information on a diskette, you cannot use FORMAT /s to put the system on pre-programmed or application diskettes. Many of these diskettes cannot be copied to customized diskettes because they are "copy protected." But, by using SYS, you can have the system on most of these diskettes.

Just like the /s switch in FORMAT, SYS transfers two *hidden files* to the specified diskette. You can't see these files, but don't worry, MS-DOS knows if they are there. System files occupy a unique position on the diskette; they are always located in the first track, at the very beginning of the diskette. Even if the files are not on the diskette, MS-DOS allocates this space to them when you format the diskette. When you use the SYS command, you put the system in this already available location. Most pre-programmed or application diskettes are produced with this pre-defined location for the system files. If you save data to a formatted diskette, this reserved area will be written over and you will not be able to transfer the system files successfully.

SYS transfers the hidden files but, unlike the /s switch, it does not transfer any of MS-DOS's command files. To have a diskette that is self-booting, *you* must also transfer the COMMAND.COM portion of the operating system. First use SYS to put the system on the diskette and then use COPY to transfer the COMMAND.COM file. You may also use COPY to transfer other files that you use a great deal, such as FORMAT.COM or DISKCOPY.COM.

Putting the System on a Diskette

Using FORMAT/s
On a blank diskette, FORMAT/s transfers the COMMAND.COM file and two "hidden files."

Using SYS
On a blank diskette, SYS transfers two "hidden files." Use the COPY command to transfer the COMMAND.COM file.

Since SYS is an external command, you must have your system diskette in drive A before issuing the command. Don't forget to put your target diskette in drive B.

```
A>sys b: <ENTER>
```

MS-DOS tells you when the transfer has been completed.

```
System transferred
A>
```

When you look at the directory of this diskette, you will see that COMMAND.COM is now one of its files. But how can you be sure that the hidden files were also transferred? The next command gives you that information.

The CHKDSK Command

use: checks the condition of the file allocation table and directories on a diskette

switches: /f   fixes the file allocation table if there are errors
                     /v   gives more explanation of error (verbose)

examples: chkdsk
                   chkdsk b:/f
                   chkdsk b:/v

This command is used to check the status or condition of any specific diskette. CHKDSK is useful for finding out exactly how much room is taken up on a diskette, how much room is still available, and what types of files are currently on the diskette. As a nice extra, CHKDSK also reports on how much memory is taken up and how much is still free, but this has nothing to do with the diskette itself.

As the name implies, you use CHKDSK to find out if everything is okay on a diskette. This is especially useful if you are having trouble using a diskette and want to try and locate the problem and save the information.

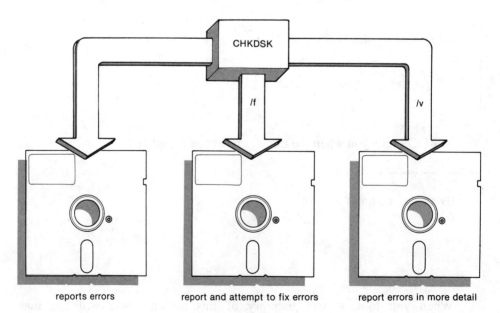

reports errors   report and attempt to fix errors   report errors in more detail

The CHKDSK command.

The first thing CHKDSK examines is the file allocation table (FAT). MS-DOS uses the FAT to keep track of the available space on a diskette. The FAT records where a file is on the diskette; it's rather like a table of contents. It also records unused space on the diskette. MS-DOS tries to make the most out of each diskette, so it does not like to have wasted space, or noncontiguous files. CHKDSK checks on space allocation and reports any problems to you.

Since CHKDSK is an external command, you must have your system diskette in a drive to use it. To check on the status of a diskette, just enter the command and the drive indicator. Let's run a CHKDSK on the system diskette:

```
A>chkdsk a: <ENTER>
```

Here is the resulting display (of a "typical" system diskette):

```
     179712 bytes total disk space
      22016 bytes in 2 hidden files
     126464 bytes in 23 user files
      31232 bytes available on disk

     262144 bytes total memory
     237568 bytes free
```

This diskette seems to be in good shape. CHKDSK gives us lots of information on the status of the diskette. We know how much total disk space is taken up, how many files are on the diskette, and how much space is still available. This is followed by the information on memory. Of course, all these numbers depend on the specifics of your computer system.

The second line of the display gives the information on hidden files. Since this diskette has two hidden files, it is reasonable to assume that the system is on this diskette. Remember that FORMAT/s and SYS transfer two hidden files when the system is placed on a diskette.

Well, so far, our diskettes have been in good shape. Here is an example of a status report that indicates a problem:

```
A>chkdsk b: <ENTER>
```

The screen reports this condition:

```
Disk error reading FAT 1

   362496 bytes total disk space
    38912 bytes in 6 user files
   323584 bytes available on disk

   262144 bytes total memory
   237568 bytes free
```

CHKDSK encountered a problem as soon as it began reading the diskette.
Here is another status report which you might receive:

```
   362496 total disk space
        0 bytes in 1 hidden file
    10240 bytes in bad sectors
   352256 bytes available on disk

   262144 bytes total memory
   237568 bytes free
```

In this example, the problem is not in the FAT, but in the disk sectors.
CHKDSK does have the ability to attempt to correct some errors. If you
want MS-DOS to check for errors *and* attempt to repair the problem, you issue
the CHKDSK command with the /f switch. The /f switch means fix if possible:

```
A>chkdsk b:/f <ENTER>
```

If an error is found, MS-DOS asks permission to fix it. There can be many
types of errors and consequently many types of error messages. Here are two
more error messages which might result from CHKDSK:

```
xxx lost clusters found in xxx chains
Convert lost chains to files(Y/N)?
```

or:

```
Allocation error for file, size adjusted
```

When you use CHKDSK with the /f switch you will need to refer to your
computer's operating system manual to understand the error message. Your manual will also advise you about what action is appropriate for each error condition.
You may also use another switch in conjunction with the CHKDSK command. /v gives you more information about the error it has found. When you use

this switch, CHKDSK lists each directory, and the files in that directory, as part of the status report. For example:

```
A>chkdsk b:/v <ENTER>

Disk error reading FAT 1
Directory B:
    B:\SAMPLE.BAK
    B:\LETTERS.BAK
    B:\SAMPLE
    B:\LETTERS

    362496 bytes total disk space
     38912 bytes in 4 user files
    323584 bytes available on disk

    262144 bytes total memory
    237584 bytes free
```

These are example file-names within the directory.

You can combine both CHKDSK switches in one command:

```
A>chkdsk/f/v <ENTER>
```

This command not only lists the contents of the diskette, it also attempts to fix any problems noted.

It's a good idea to use CHKDSK often. Not only can it prevent minor problems from growing into major ones, but it brings you piece of mind just knowing that everything on your diskettes is "all right with the world."

The MODE Command

use: controls input/output devices

examples: mode LPT1:80,6
            mode com1:12,n,8,1,p
            mode ,r,t

The MODE command is rather unique in MS-DOS in that it has nothing to do with disks or diskettes. Instead, MODE is used to control the way your input/output devices operate. For instance, some computer systems allow you to use a printer in a variety of different ways. You use the MODE command to tell your system how to operate the printer. For example:

```
A>mode LPT1:80,6 <ENTER>
```

This may seem like gibberish to you, but MS-DOS understands it.

Broken down, this command tells MS-DOS to set the printer (LPT is the system's designation for printer) that is number 1 (some systems can have more than one printer attached at one time) so that it outputs 80-character lines, at the vertical spacing of 6 lines per inch. Don't worry about using MODE like this right now. Your operations guide describes your system's use of MODE when dealing with printers and other input/output ports.

There is one instance of using MODE that is more usual, however. This is to adjust your display screen. You are probably saying *"There's nothing wrong with my display or have I been missing something?"* Well, chances are you are right. In most situations, your display is perfectly all right. If, however, you use a Color/Graphics Monitor Adapter you may need the MODE command.

On a television set or color monitor, you may occasionally notice that the first few characters of the display line are somewhere off in the hinterland beyond the left edge of the screen. Even the prompt may be out of sight. You use the MODE command to correct this alignment problem. Assume that the prompt is there even if you can't see it:

```
A>mode ,r,t <ENTER>
```

Be especially careful when entering this command; you must leave a space after mode and put a comma *in front of the letter r* as well as a comma separating the two letters. This command is telling MS-DOS to move the display to the right. Here is how MS-DOS responds:

```
Resident portion of MODE loaded
0123456789012345678901234567890123456789012345678901234567890123456789

Do you see the leftmost 0? (Y/N)
```

If you still need to move the display to the right, enter "N". If you can see the 0 at the far left, enter "Y". It would be nice if all problems could be solved so easily.

If you can't see the characters to the far right of your screen, use MODE to move them to the left. Issue the same command, but substitute an L for the R:

```
A>mode ,1,t <ENTER>

01234567890123456789012345678901234567890123456789012345678

Do you see the rightmost 9? (Y/N)
```

Respond yes if you can see the 9, or no to move the display farther to the left. After you have adjusted the display and answered yes, MS-DOS returns you to the operating system.

In addition to setting up your printer and aligning your display, MODE can also be used for setting up additional advanced applications, such as communications. You can find this additional information in your user's manual or in the *MS-DOS Bible* (Sams P/C #22408).

Well, you have expanded your knowledge of MS-DOS rather significantly in this chapter. Not only can you now use the keyboard and special keys to edit, but you can list your files to your specification (DIR/w and DIR/p), you can FORMAT with new options (/v and /s), and you can put the system on pre-programmed diskettes (SYS). To verify that your diskettes are holding up, you can use CHKDSK and, if your display is askew, you can fix that too. In the next chapter we will present a whole new idea about how to use MS-DOS files, batch processing!

8

Mixing up a Fresh Batch

8 Mixing up a Fresh Batch

As you become more familiar with MS-DOS commands, you gain an understanding of how, when, and why to use specific commands. In fact, what you may have found at first difficult becomes increasingly routine as you employ these commands more often.

The fact is that many of the operations you perform with the computer are repetitive. You probably find yourself using certain sequences of commands, in the same pattern, over and over again. Just as the editing keys gave you one shortcut to avoid useless repetitiveness, MS-DOS has another helpmate to save you time and frustration. This new tool is called a *batch file*, and in this chapter we are going to see how batch files can make your computing more efficient.

What Are Batch Files?

Batch files are something like a cookbook for commands. They contain lists of "steps" in the form of MS-DOS commands that combine to produce one result. After this "recipe" is established, the batch file gives you the same result every time you run it. The "ingredients" in a batch file are data files. These may change from time to time, but the product of the batch file is still the same. A real-life example may explain this further.

There is a standard commodity in everyone's life called "bread." But bread does not just spring full grown from the earth. What is called bread is really a combination of wheat, liquid, and flavoring that, mixed together, is recognized as bread. When you make bread, the ingredients may vary. You can use whole wheat or white flour; you may include water or milk; you may add raisins or caraway seeds. The steps, however, in making bread always follow a specific pattern. First you measure, then you combine, then you knead, and finally you bake. The result is bread. A recipe for bread is a shortcut most cooks use because it defines *what* and *how much* and *in what order*. Not only does this reduce mistakes, it makes the process go faster because the procedure is already laid out; you just follow the instructions. When you want to eat a piece of bread, you simply ask: give me some bread. Since bread already exists you just cut off a slice; you don't have to go out and cut the wheat, then grind the flour, and so on.

Batch files perform a similar service for MS-DOS users. You enter a series of commands, the "recipe" that, when executed in order, provides specific results. The product is always the same because you follow the same steps each time. The "ingredients" may change however. Even if you enter different filenames, the commands still perform in the same order. And since all of these commands are stored in one file, identified by a "batch filename," you can use this formula over and over again, simply by entering the batch filename. Not only is this faster than entering each of the commands separately, it also eliminates mistakes since the commands are already correctly entered in the batch file. The batch file is already "made up."

sequence of instructions + ingredients   = bread

series of commands   + data filenames = batch file

For all you commuters, who never understood cooking anyway, here is another analogy. Batch files are like a car pool. When everybody drives his own car, each commuter takes up space on the freeway although their destination may be the same. All drive independently and all do eventually arrive at work. But when the commuters join in a car pool, there is a saving of space, time, and money. The same result occurs, all workers arrive at work, but the method of getting there is more efficient. Batch files are like a car pool for commands. You only need one driver and one vehicle, but the result is the same. The identical actions are performed by the commands, but there is a saving in space and time.

Batch files are ASCII text files, just like the files you use when you work with typical MS-DOS commands such as DIR, COPY, and TYPE. The files you use most frequently hold various kinds of information, data, programs, or operating system commands. Batch files contain commands, plus some explanatory statements. How much a batch file can do is dependent on how many commands you enter. Batch files are most useful when they perform a sequence of commands that you use very frequently.

Here is one example of the convenience of batch files. You may find that you frequently perform the following sequence of events (I do this whenever I want to backup files and see the contents of each file). First you format a diskette, then you copy files to it, then you ask for a directory of the diskette, and finally you look at one or more of the files to check the contents. This procedure can be done by entering four commands: FORMAT, COPY, DIR, and TYPE. You can enter each of these commands separately, repeating the drive designations and filenames each time. But you can save yourself time, and eliminate the inevitable typing errors, by putting all these commands in one batch file. To execute this batch file all you do in enter one command, the name of the batch file. Does this sound confusing? Let's review your normal procedure.

First you enter the FORMAT command:

```
format b:
```

After the diskette is formatted you enter:

```
copy a:datafile b:
```

When the copy is completed you ask for a directory:

```
dir b:
```

And finally, you list the contents of the file:

```
type b:datafile
```

Now let's see how you can put all these commands in one batch file.

Creating a Batch File from Scratch

Before you can follow a recipe it has to be written down. Putting a series of commands in a batch file is simple. The rules for a batch filename are the same as for other filenames, but in a batch file you must include the extension ".BAT".

To run through this exercise on batch files, take on the role of a computer "baker." The goodie you are going to whip up is a practice file called "datafile". For brevity's sake, this file will contain only one line: "This is a demonstration batch file." Since this is an ASCII file, you can use EDLIN to create this data file.

EDLIN is on your system diskette as the file "EDLIN.COM". Your "datafile" will also be on the system diskette. Put this diskette in drive A and call up EDLIN.

```
A>edlin datafile <ENTER>
New file
*i <ENTER>
      1:*This is a demonstration batch file. <ENTER>
      2:*^C

*e <ENTER>
```

This file is going to be the "generic" data file in our example. It stands for any files you might want to use in the batch file.

A Choice of Cooking Methods

Up until now, using EDLIN was the only method you knew for creating a file. But there is an alternative way to create files, using the COPY commands. You are going to use both methods to create your batch file.

As is true whenever you use EDLIN, you must be sure the system diskette you are using contains the EDLIN.COM file. This diskette is probably still in drive A from the creation of "datafile" in the previous example. Use it now to combine the ingredients in your master batch file "copydata.bat":

```
A>edlin copydata.bat <ENTER>          The filename must
                                      contain the .bat
                                      extension.
New file
*i <ENTER>
      1:*format b: <ENTER>            Enter one command
      2:*copy a:datafile b: <ENTER>   per line.
      3:*dir b: <ENTER>
      4:*type b:datafile <ENTER>
      5:*^C

*e <ENTER>
```

Each command is entered on a separate line. This is the standard EDLIN procedure. The only difference is that your filename contains the "BAT" extension. This batch file assumes that the diskette in drive B is unformatted (line number 1). It "believes" that the data you want to copy ("datafile") is on the diskette in drive A, and that you want to copy this file to the diskette on drive B (line number 2). You then want to check the directory for the existence of the file (line number 3) and type out the contents of the file (line number 4).

Another way to create a file is to type the information directly into a file using the COPY commands. To do this you use COPY in conjunction with the

CON device name. CON is one of those reserved device names that MS-DOS uses to recognize parts of the computer system. CON stands for console (your keyboard). When you use COPY CON, you tell MS-DOS to COPY all the information you are typing in on your keyboard and put it directly into a file. The advantage of using COPY CON is that you do not have to have EDLIN on the diskette to create the file. The disadvantage is that you cannot edit a line in a COPY CON file after you have pressed <ENTER>.

To create "copydata.bat" using COPY CON enter the commands in sequence. There are no line numbers when using COPY CON. Again, enter one command per line:

```
A>copy con: copydata.bat <ENTER>
format b: <ENTER>
copy a:datafile b: <ENTER>
dir b: <ENTER>
type b:datafile <ENTER>
^Z <ENTER>
```
                                        ^Z (Ctrl Z) is the end of file
                                        marker.

After you enter the end of file marker, MS-DOS responds:

```
1 File(s) copied
```

The file has been copied onto the diskette in drive A. This is indicated by the fact that A> is the current drive. Creating a batch file using COPY does not cause any of the commands *within* the file to be executed. To MS-DOS they are just like any other text. The "1 File(s) copied" message means that this created file is now stored on the diskette in drive A.

Two Ways To Create a Batch File	
Using EDLIN	**Using COPY CON:**
external command (you need the system diskette)	internal command (you don't need the system diskette)
you can edit lines within the file	you can't edit a line in the file if you've already pressed <ENTER>

How Do You Use a Batch File?

Starting a Batch File

Now that you have created the batch file, what do you do with it? Well, from now on, anytime you want to perform this FORMAT-COPY-DIR-TYPE sequence, you simply type in the name of the batch file in response to the MS-DOS prompt. Of course, you must have the diskette containing the batch file and any files to be copied in the correct drive. The sequence of commands is executed automatically. MS-DOS shows you each command as it is processed. The appearance is the same as if you were entering each command separately:

```
A>copydata <ENTER>      Enter the batch filename. You do not need to
                        include the extension.
```

The batch file begins executing:

```
A>format b:
```
This is the first command in your batch file.

```
Insert new diskette for drive B:
and strike any key when ready
```
All messages associated with the FORMAT command appear automatically. You must strike a key here for the file to continue processing.

```
Formatting...Format complete

    362496 bytes total disk space
    362496 bytes available on disk
```

```
Format another (Y/N)?n
```
Again, you must respond to all command requests for input.

```
A>copy a:datafile b:
```
Next, MS-DOS copies the file.

```
    1 File(s) copied
```

```
A>dir b:
```
MS-DOS automatically continues with the third command in the batch file.

```
    Volume in drive B has no label
    Directory of B:\
```
The normal messages associated with DIR are displayed.

```
DATAFILE            38    12-17-84   11:35a
            1 File(s)        361472 bytes free
```

```
A>type b:datafile
```
MS-DOS now executes the fourth command in the batch file.

```
This is a demonstration batch file.
```
Here are the contents of "datafile".

```
A>
```
When the batch file is finished, MS-DOS returns to the prompt.

Running a Batch File

1. Create a batch file with **EDLIN** or **COPY.CON**.

2. Name the file with a **.BAT** extension.

3. To run the file, enter the filename (.BAT is not necessary).

When you run your first batch file you will be amazed at how quickly the commands happen. You may even feel a lack of control watching messages and commands appear on the screen. But MS-DOS keeps you informed of what it is doing each step of the way. Each command is displayed as the batch file reaches it, and all messages and queries associated with the command are displayed during processing. The difference is that you can just sit back and observe!

This is the wonder of batch processing. With the simple input of one file-name, and a response to the "strike key" and "FORMAT another" queries, you have formatted a disk, copied a file, displayed a directory, and typed out the contents of a file. And MS-DOS has returned to await your next command.

You can execute several batch files in a row. To do this, simply make the last command in a batch file the name of another batch file. For example, suppose we had two batch files: "copydata" and "erasedat". "Erasedat" might be a batch file to clean up a diskette after all the needed files had been copied. The last command line of "copydata" would contain the name "erasedat". This is how your modified "copydata.bat" would appear:

```
format b:
copy a:datafile b:
dir b:
type b:datafile          Last command to be executed.
erasedat.bat             Call this batch file.
```

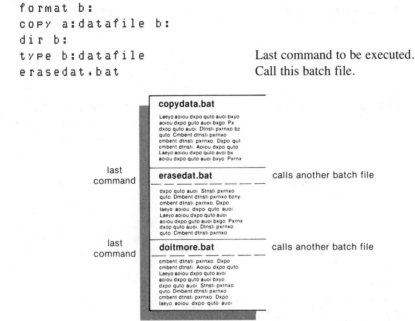

Superbatch.

When you call another batch file from within a file, the processing continues with the first command in the new file. This is a one-way street, however. You can't return to "copydata" once you begin processing "erasedat". These files are *chained* one to the other.

This example is a simple illustration of how useful batch files can be. You are probably already beginning to fashion your own batch files to eliminate the drudgery of certain sequences of operations you perform quite frequently.

Stopping a Batch File

Occasionally you may find yourself in the middle of a batch file and you want to stop the processing. Perhaps you realize that you don't have time to complete the batch file, you want to use different data diskettes, or you don't want a series of chained batch files to execute. Whatever the reason, MS-DOS allows you the option of stopping batch files in the middle of an operation. Another name for "executing batch files" is "batch processing." You stop batch processing just like you interrupt any on-going operation on the computer, you press ^C or <Ctrl> <Break>. When a batch file is processing and you press ^C, MS-DOS displays this message:

```
Terminate batch job (Y/N)?
```

A "Y" answer tells DOS to ignore the rest of the commands in the batch file and return you to the DOS prompt. An "N" answer tells DOS to terminate processing of the *current* command, but to continue processing with the next command in the batch file.

For example, while processing the "copydata" file, you may not want to see the entire directory of the diskette. Therefore, you would press <Ctrl> <Break> while the DIR command was processing, and then type "N" in response to the terminate question. Processing would continue with the TYPE command.

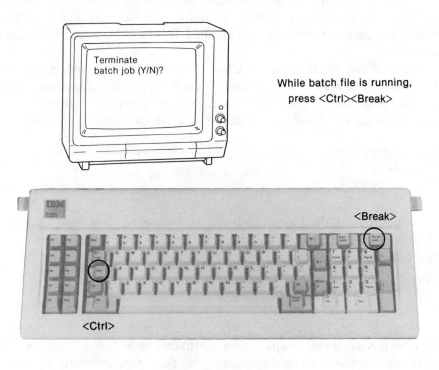

Stopping a batch file.

Adding More Ingredients

Often you may want to perform the same sequence of commands on different sets of files. In the initial version of "copydata", you were only able to copy one file, "datafile". But this situation is very limiting. It means that, whenever you want to copy some other file besides "datafile", you need to create a new batch file containing the new filename. Obviously this limits the time-saving capabilities of batch files. But MS-DOS has provided for this situation by allowing you to use *replaceable parameters* in batch files.

A parameter is the part of a command that indicates what the command is to be performed "on." Usually this is the name of the file that will be affected by the command. The command "copy a:datafile b:" consists of the actual command name "copy" and the parameters that identify *on what,* that is, on the file in drive A called "datafile". "Datafile" is a parameter of this command.

Replaceable parameters are "dummies." That doesn't mean that they sit in the corner and wear funny hats. It does mean that they are simply symbols that stand for the actual names of real files. In batch files, replaceable parameters are indicated by the percent sign (%) followed by a number, for example, %1, %2. The actual files that replace these symbols are specified when you call the batch file. The name of the file to replace %1 follows the batch file name; the file to replace %2 comes next on the command line. This probably sounds a bit confusing at first.

Imagine that you have created a batch file to display the contents of several files. You want to use this file over and over again, but you will type out different files each time, so you create the batch file using replaceable parameters. The name of this file is "typeit.bat". Within the file are these three commands:

```
type %1
type %2
type %3
```

When you call the file you indicate the files to be substituted for the %1, %2, and %3 parameters by listing them, in order, on the command line. Leave a space between parameters.

```
typeit chap1 chap2 chap3
```

When MS-DOS encounters the first dummy parameter, %1, it substitutes chap1 for this parameter. chap2 is then substituted for %2, and chap3 for %3. If the file also contained another command using these parameters, for example:

```
copy %1
copy %2
copy %3
```

then chap1, chap2, and chap3 would again be substituted. The replaceable parameters will have the same values throughout the batch file.

```
Replaceable Parameters

type %1
type %2      The parameters listed after the filename are substituted whenever
type %3      %1, %2, or %3 are called for in the batch file.
copy %1
copy %2
copy %3
```

You can have up to ten replaceable parameters (%0-%9) in a batch file. It is possible to have more; see the SHIFT command later in this chapter for ways to get around this limitation. %0 is reserved for the name of the batch file itself. Thus, typing %0 in the file above would cause MS-DOS to type out the "typeit" file itself.

Replaceable parameters can be used in any batch file. Just remember that you must specify what files are to be substituted for the dummy parameters when you call the file.

You can use all of the MS-DOS commands in a batch file. But, in addition, there are specific *batch commands* (or *subcommands*) that are only used in batch files.

Commands in Batch Processing

The ECHO Command

use: turns on or off the echoing of commands to the screen, or displays messages when ECHO is off

examples: echo on
            echo off
            echo Here are the contents of datafile

The concept of echoing is not new to you. We discussed echoing in a different context earlier when we used the editing keys ^P and ^N to control the echoing of the screen to the printer. Here the same type of echoing is meant, but we are talking about echoing the commands *within a batch file to the screen.*

Normally, the ECHO command is in the ON mode. In the ON mode, each command is echoed (displayed) on the screen as that command is processing. The display of each command can be useful when you want to keep close track of what is happening inside a batch file. But this echoing feature can also be bothersome when you don't need it, cluttering up the screen with useless information.

If you don't want to see each command displayed on the screen, you can set ECHO to the OFF mode. When ECHO is OFF, the commands themselves do not appear on the screen, but all messages associated with the commands are still displayed. To eliminate echoing, enter this command prior to any commands you don't want to see. For example, if we wanted to include ECHO OFF in our "copydata" file, we would enter it first:

```
A>copy con: copydata.bat <ENTER>
echo off <ENTER>
format b: <ENTER>
copy a:datafile b: <ENTER>
dir b: <ENTER>
type b:datafile <ENTER>
^Z <ENTER>

    1 File(s) copied
```

When you run this version of "copydata" you will not see any command lines on the screen after the initial ECHO OFF command:

```
A>copydata <ENTER>
A>echo off                                This first command tells
                                          you ECHO is OFF.
Insert new diskette for drive B:          Command messages still
and strike any key when ready             appear.
                                          Press a key to continue.


Formatting...Format complete

    362496 bytes total disk space
    362496 bytes available on disk

Format another (Y/N)?n                    You answer n.

  1 File(s) copied
```

```
Volume in drive B has no label    DIR output is displayed.
Directory of B:\

DATAFILE               38    11-20-84    11:49a
        1 File(s)             361472 bytes free
This is a demonstration batch file.   Here is the result of the
                                      TYPE command.

A>
```

If, at some point in the batch file, you again wanted to see the echoing of each command as it was processed, you would enter a new ECHO command, ECHO ON. All subsequent commands would then appear on the screen.

ECHO has another option which allows you to put messages on the screen, even when ECHO is in the OFF mode. Although you will not see the commands, you will see the message. Let's set the ECHO OFF in our "copydata" batch file, but include a message we do want to see displayed.

```
A>copy con: copydata.bat <ENTER>
echo off <ENTER>
format b: <ENTER>
copy a:datafile b: <ENTER>
dir b: <ENTER>
echo Here are the contents of datafile: <ENTER>
type b:datafile <ENTER>
^Z <ENTER>
```

The results of this batch file are exactly the same as the last example until the DIR listing has been displayed. Then our message is echoed:

```
DATAFILE              38     11-20-84    11:49a
       1 File(s)            361472 bytes free
Here are the contents of datafile:
This is a demonstration batch file.

A>
```

If you enter ECHO with no parameters, MS-DOS displays the current status of ECHO (ON or OFF). Use ECHO to decide which commands you want to see during batch file processing and to give yourself helpful messages regardless of the status of the ECHO command.

The REM Command

use: puts comments into a batch file

example: rem This file checks disks

The REM (REMark) command is used, like the ECHO command, to put comments into a batch file. These can be statements to you (or any user of the batch file) that explain what the file does or what is happening at a specific moment. REM statements are affected by the status of ECHO. When ECHO is in the OFF mode, REM statements are not displayed in the same way that commands are not displayed.

REM commands can contain any information you think will help you understand the batch file better. You can also use REM to insert blank lines in a file. The following batch file, "newdisk", formats and puts the system on new diskettes. It then checks the condition of the diskette:

```
A> copy con: newdisk.bat <ENTER>
rem This file formats and checks new disks.<ENTER>
rem The system will be put on the diskette.<ENTER>
format b:/s <ENTER>
dir b: <ENTER>
rem Here is the condition of this diskette.<ENTER>
chkdsk b: <ENTER>
rem This diskette is ready to use, don't forget to label it! <ENTER>
^Z <ENTER>

        1 File(s) copied
```

To run "newdisk" enter the filename:

```
A>newdisk <ENTER>
```

This is what you will see on the screen:

```
A>rem This file formats and checks new disks.

A>rem The system will be put on the diskette.

A>format b:/s
Insert new diskette for drive B:
and strike any key when ready        You press a key.

Formatting...Format complete
System transferred

    362496 bytes total disk space
     40960 bytes used by system
    321536 bytes available on disk

Format another (Y/N)?n              You answer n.
A>dir b:

    Volume in drive B has no label
    Directory of B:\

COMMAND   COM    17664  3-08-83   12:00p
        1 File(s)   321536 bytes free

A>rem Here is the condition of this diskette.

A>chkdsk b:

    362496 bytes total disk space
     22528 bytes in 2 hidden files
     18432 bytes in 1 user files
    321536 bytes available on disk

    262144 bytes total memory
    237456 bytes free


A>rem This diskette is ready to use, don't forget to label it!


A>
```

You can see from this example how the addition of REM statements can help clarify the contents and operations of a batch file. If you wish, you could use the ECHO OFF mode to eliminate the display of all command lines, but remember this will also eliminate the display of all REM statements.

Comparison of ECHO and REMark

	ECHO		REMark
ON	Commands are displayed	**ECHO ON**	REM statements are
OFF	Commands are not dis-		displayed
	played but messages still	**ECHO OFF**	REM statements are
	appear		not displayed

The PAUSE Command

use: temporarily halts the processing of a batch file

example: pause Remove the diskette currently in drive B.

The PAUSE command puts a built-in stop into a batch file. You use this command when you need to *do* something before the next command is executed, such as change a diskette or turn on the printer. You might also use PAUSE to allow a full screen to be read before proceeding to the next screen.

Since you stop processing with the PAUSE command, you must then press a key to continue the batch file. As part of the PAUSE command, MS-DOS has an automatic message which appears after the PAUSE command—"Strike any key when ready." You don't need to add this message, it will always appear after a PAUSE command. Here is how PAUSE might be incorporated into our "newdisk" batch file:

```
A>copy con: newdisk.bat <ENTER>
rem This file formats and checks new disks.<ENTER>
pause Remove the diskette currently in drive B. <ENTER>
rem The system will be put on the diskette.<ENTER>
format b:/s <ENTER>
dir b: <ENTER>
rem Here is the condition of this diskette.<ENTER>
chkdsk b: <ENTER>
```

```
rem This diskette is ready to use, don't forget to label it! <ENTER>
^Z <ENTER>


        1 File(s) copied
```

Here is how you see this version of "newdisk":

```
A>rem This file formats and checks new disks.

A>pause Remove the diskette currently in drive B.
Strike a key when ready . . .                   You press a key.

A>rem The system will be put on the diskette.

A>format b:/s
Insert new diskette for drive B:
and strike any key when ready

Formatting...Format complete
System transferred

   362496 bytes total disk space
    40960 bytes used by system
   321536 bytes available on disk

Format another (Y/N)?n                          You answer n.
A>dir b:

   Volume in drive B has no label
   Directory of B:\

COMMAND  COM    17664   3-08-83   12:00p
        1 File(s)     321536 bytes free

A>rem Here is the condition of this diskette.

A>chkdsk b:

   362496 bytes total disk space
    22528 bytes in 2 hidden files
    18432 bytes in 1 user files
   321536 bytes available on disk

   262144 bytes total memory
   237456 bytes free
```

```
A>rem This diskette is ready to use, don't forget to label it!
A>
```

PAUSE is useful as a safety device within a batch file. In this case you use it as a warning, so you will be sure not to format over a diskette that contains data. This warning can be very effective in helping you avoid those heart-wrenching errors that we all make at one time or another. For example, you might have included in a batch file the command to erase all old files. Inserting a pause command could save you from a frustrating mistake:

```
dir b:
pause Make sure all desired files have been copied, or BREAK,
del oldfiles
```

The GOTO Command

use: transfers processing to a specified location defined by a label

example: GOTO :repeat

The GOTO command works in conjunction with a *label*. The label is any name you choose that identifies a location in a batch file, rather like the way a line number in EDLIN indicates a location. The label is preceded by a colon (:). GOTO transfers control of the processing to the line *after* the label.

GOTO is a convenient command when you want to keep repeating a certain activity without changing any parameters. Suppose you had a letter and needed

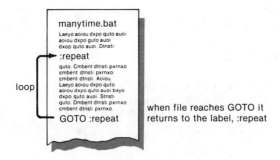

The GOTO command

several duplicates made. You could set up a batch file, using GOTO, to type out as many duplicates as you needed.

When you use GOTO with a label designation, you create a *loop*. A loop is an operation that will keep repeating until you stop it. To escape from a loop in a batch file, use ^C or <Ctrl> <Break> to terminate the job. The loop itself is not displayed on the screen.

The name of this batch file is "manytime.bat". The label which defines where the command returns is called ":repeat".

```
A>copy con:manytime.bat <ENTER>
rem This file makes duplicate copies of a letter. <ENTER>
echo off <ENTER>
copy a:letter b: <ENTER>
:repeat <ENTER>
type b:letter <ENTER>
echo Press CTRL BREAK to stop this batch file. <ENTER>
goto :repeat <ENTER>
^Z <ENTER>

        1 File(s) copied
```

To run this batch file you must have the file "letter" on the diskette in drive A, along with the "manytime.bat" file. For our example, the file "letter" contains one line, "This is a sample for the goto command". To execute "manytime" enter the name of the batch file:

```
A>manytime <ENTER>
```

"Manytime" results in this display:

```
A>rem This file makes duplicate copies of a letter.

A>echo off
        1 File(s) copied
```

```
This is a sample for the goto command.
Press CTRL BREAK to stop this batch file.
This is a sample for the goto command.
Press CTRL BREAK to stop this batch file.
This is a sample for the goto command.
Press CTRL BREAK to stop this batch file.
                   .
                   .
                   .
```

These messages continue to be displayed until you stop processing by pressing <Ctrl> <Break>.

The IF Command

use: transfers processing to a specified location depending on a condition

example: IF condition

           There are three conditions:
           IF exist
           IF string 1 = = string 2
           IF errorlevel

The IF command tells the batch file to continue processing the next command if a certain condition is *true*. The condition can be one of three options. The first is *IF exist*. IF exist uses a file specification as the test. If the file exists (the condition is true), then processing passes to the specified GOTO location. If the file does not exist (the condition is false), then batch processing continues with the next command.

For our "IF exist" example, let's create a batch file that duplicates a letter until it is instructed to stop, just like our "manytime" batch file. But this batch file contains another instruction. It tells MS-DOS to check first to see if the letter has been copied from A to B. If the letter does not exist on B, the batch file formats the diskette in B, copies the file to B, makes sure the file is on B by listing a directory, and then starts the duplication process. If the file already exists on B, the letter has been copied and duplication begins immediately. Here are the contents of the "copylet" batch file:

```
A>copy con: copylet.bat <ENTER>
echo off <ENTER>
if exist b:letter goto :exists <ENTER>
format b: <ENTER>
copy a:letter b: <ENTER>
dir b: <ENTER>
:exists <ENTER>
type b:letter <ENTER>
echo Press CTRL BREAK to stop this batch file. <ENTER>
goto :exists <ENTER>
^Z <ENTER>

    1 File(s) copied
```

Here are the results of the first run of "copylet":

```
A>copylet <ENTER>

A>echo off
Insert new diskette for drive B:
and strike any key when ready        The "letter" file was not
                                     found on the B diskette so
                                     formatting begins.


Formatting...Format complete

   362496 bytes total disk space
   362496 bytes available on disk

Format another (Y/N)?n              1 File(s)copied

                                     You answer n, MS-DOS
                                     proceeds to copy the file to
                                     B.


   Volume in drive B has no label
   Directory of B:\                  MS-DOS lists the
                                     directory.

LETTER          40  11-20-84  12:54P
     1 File(s)    361472 bytes free
```

```
This is a sample for the goto command,      TYPE
Press CTRL BREAK to stop this batch file, command
This is a sample for the goto command,      executes.
Press CTRL BREAK to stop this batch file, ECHO
This is a sample for the goto command,      message.
Press CTRL BREAK to stop this batch file,
This is a sample for the goto command,
Press CTRL BREAK to stop this batch file, The file is
This is a sample for the goto command,      now in the
Press CTRL BREAK to stop this batch file, :exists loop.
This is a sample ,,,
```

The first time you run "copylet" the "letter" file will not be found on the B diskette unless it had been copied previously. The batch file checks for this condition. Not finding the file on the indicated diskette, it proceeds to format the diskette, copy the file, and give you a directory. Duplication then continues until you halt the batch file.

Provided you use the same diskette in drive B, the results will be different the second time you run "copylet":

```
A>copylet <ENTER>

A>echo off
This is a sample for the goto command,
Press CTRL BREAK to stop this batch file,
This is a sample for the goto command,
Press CTRL BREAK to stop this batch file,
This is ,,,
```

On all consequent runs of "copylet", the condition is true (the "letter" file already exists on drive B). Therefore, the batch file skips directly to the :exists loop and begins duplicating the letter. This continues until you terminate the batch file.

The second IF option uses a *string* as a test. A string is simply computereze for *a group of characters*. In this IF command you tell DOS to go to a specific location or perform a certain operation when the strings match (the condition is true). When you enter the strings into the command, they are separated by two equal signs (= =). For example, we might have a batch file with replaceable parameters. It contains this command:

```
IF %1 == Seamus echo Seamus is ready.
```

Whenever Seamus was entered as the %1 parameter, this condition would be true, and the echo command "Seamus is ready" would be displayed. However, if Matt was entered as the %1 parameter, then the condition would be false and the echo message would not appear.

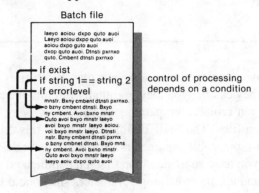

The IF command.

The third IF option uses ERRORLEVEL as the test. ERRORLEVEL is an indicator (sometimes called a *flag*) that signals the status of a certain condition. ERRORLEVEL is internally set as a part of certain MS-DOS commands. It indicates whether an operation was sucessfully performed. ERRORLEVEL 1 indicates failure of the operation, ERRORLEVEL 0 indicates successful completion of the command.

Imagine that you had a program that copied all files from one diskette to another. This "copyall" file includes these commands:

```
copy a:*.* b:
if errorlevel 1  echo copyall failure
dir b:
```

The message "copyall failure" appears on the screen whenever all the files are not sucessfully copied. Non-completion of the operation is this case makes the condition true. The message does not appear when all the files are copied because this results in an ERRORLEVEL of 0 and the IF condition is false.

These IF commands may seem a bit complicated at first. Take your time and go slowly as you begin to use this command. A few practice sessions will up your confidence level tremendously. You will discover very quickly just how useful the IF command can be in making your batch commands do *exactly* what you need them to do.

The SHIFT Command

use: allows more than ten replaceable parameters in a batch file

example: shift

After you have developed some of your own batch files and have seen just how time-saving they can be, you may eventually run into the problem of wanting to use more than ten replaceable parameters. You may want to type out twelve files or copy fifteen files. The SHIFT command solves this dilemma by allowing you to exceed ten replaceable parameters. You can't just add %11, %12, and so on. Instead, after you have substituted the first ten parameters, your %1 parameter drops off the list and all the remaining parameters shift one position to the left.

Suppose you want to create a batch file to display the letters of the alphabet up to and including the letter L. This means there are twelve parameters you want substituted into the file. This is how the contents of "alphabet" appear:

```
echo off
echo %0 %1 %2 %3 %4 %5 %6 %7 %8 %9
SHIFT
echo %0 %1 %2 %3 %4 %5 %6 %7 %8 %9
SHIFT
echo %0 %1 %2 %3 %4 %5 %6 %7 %8 %9
SHIFT
echo %0 %1 %2 %3 %4 %5 %6 %7 %8 %9
SHIFT
```

You execute this file by calling the batch file:

```
A>alphabet A B C D E F G H I J K L <ENTER>
```

The first time you use parameters in your batch file, the first ten parameters are substituted just as they were entered. But after the SHIFT command, all the parameters would move over one space to the left. The leftmost parameter is dropped and the new parameter (number 10 in the list) is moved into the %9 position. This move to the left continues each time you issue the SHIFT command.

The output of "alphabet" looks like this:

```
A>echo off
alphabet A B C D E G F G H I
A B C D E F G H I J
B C D E F G H I J K
C D E F G H I J K L
```

You can easily see how you could continue substituting parameters until all that you included have been displayed. Once there are less than ten parameters left, the spaces to the right will be left blank.

The FOR Command

use: allows repetition of the same command on a series of files

example: for %%A in (chap1.txt chap2.txt chap3.txt) do dir %%A

This batch command uses a few new concepts. The first is *set*. A set is a group of files that follow the "in" portion of the FOR command. Thus, the set in our example above is chap1.txt, chap2.txt, and chap3.txt. Immediately following the FOR command is a *variable,* designated with two percent signs (%%) and a name. This variable also follows the "do" section of the command. The FOR command allows you to repeat an action or operation for each of the files contained in the set.

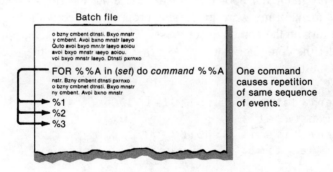

The FOR Command.

Suppose you want to create a batch file to check for the existence of files on a diskette, in this case, three files named chap1, chap2, and chap3. Here is how the FOR command can accomplish this:

```
for %%A in (chap1.txt chap2.txt chap3.txt) do dir %%A
```

If the files are found, these three results are displayed:

```
dir chap1.txt
dir chap2.txt
dir chap3.txt
```

You can make this command even more powerful by using wildcards for the set. Here is an easy, fast way to copy all the files on a diskette:

```
for %%B in (*.*) do copy %%B
```

Putting It on Automatic

Up to now when you created batch files, each has been given its own unique name. There is one type of batch file that comes pre-named and it performs one very specific and very useful function. This is the AUTOEXEC.BAT file.

AUTOEXEC.BAT is designed to make starting up the computer more efficient. When you boot the system, MS-DOS automatically examines the contents of the boot diskette. If it finds an AUTOEXEC.BAT file on the diskette, it immediately executes this command first. Thus, by putting an AUTOEXEC.BAT file on your boot diskette, you can go directly to the program you want. For instance, most of the time when I use my computer, I want to use the word-processing program. If I booted normally, these are the steps I take to arrive at the opening menu of my word-processing program, called with the letters ws.

First I turn on the computer (or press <Ctrl> <Alt> <Del> if it is a warm boot) and let the computer start up. My first message after the boot is the time and date requests:

```
Current date is Tue 1 01-1980
Enter new date:
Current time is 0:00:00
Enter new time:
```

After responding to these requests, the opening screen is shown:

```
The XYZ Personal Computer DOS
Version 2.0 (C) Copyright XYZ Company, 1981,1982

A>
```

Now at this point I remove the system diskette, insert my word-processing diskette, and call the file I want: ws.

But by using AUTOEXEC.BAT I can arrive at this same point with only one entry. My AUTOEXEC.BAT contains only two lines, the ECHO OFF command and the name of the file I want to go to:

```
A>copy con: autoexec.bat <ENTER>
echo off <ENTER>
ws <ENTER>
^Z <ENTER>
```

Of course, to make this work, I have to first put the system on my word-processing diskette so I can boot using this diskette. The AUTOEXEC.BAT file must also be on this diskette.

Now to get to my word-processing program I simply start the system. Like magic, the opening menu appears with no further input from me.

Here is how AUTOEXEC.BAT could be used to move you right into a BASIC program:

```
A>copy con: autoexec.bat <ENTER>
echo off <ENTER>
basica b:begin <ENTER>
^Z <ENTER>
```

When you boot, the BASICA interpreter on drive A is loaded into the computer, followed by the "begin.bas" program on drive B, which would then begin to run. All you have to do is be sure the correct diskettes are in the correct drives.

AUTOEXEC.BAT files skip over the time and date requests. If you want to use AUTOEXEC.BAT and still enter this information, just include the TIME and DATE commands in your AUTOEXEC.BAT file.

One note of caution: you can only have one AUTOEXEC.BAT file on a diskette. Since each file must have a unique name, you are limited to one AUTOEXEC.BAT. If you try to create more than one AUTOEXEC.BAT file, the previous AUTOEXEC.BAT will be erased as you enter the new data.

Well, this chapter on batch files and batch processing surely marks your entry into the world of the "how did I live without this" computer user. Up until now you have been easing your way into MS-DOS knowledge. From this point on you will begin using that knowledge to make the computer work for you.

In this chapter you were introduced to batch files and batch processing. You learned that you can create files using both the EDLIN program and the COPY CON command. Each of the batch commands, ECHO, REM, PAUSE, GOTO, IF, SHIFT, and FOR, was explained. The creation of an AUTOEXEC.BAT file and some common uses of this type of file were explored. Batch processing is an area that you will continue to develop as you find your own uses for this special feature of MS-DOS.

Of course, the more you work with your computer, the more files you create and need to store and retrieve. Some of your diskettes may be pretty confusing by now and your directories are probably becoming a maze of names. Well, take heart. In the next chapter you are going to learn how to organize those directories so you can find what you want, when you want it.

9

You Can See
the Forest for the Trees

- Directly on the Path in Front of You
- Getting to the Root of the Matter
- Subdirectories and Pathnames
- Special Pathmarkers
- Getting Back to Your Roots
    - Keeping Current
- Finding the Right Home for a File
- Blazing New Trails
- The Path of Least Resistance
    - Taking a Shortcut
- Climbing around in the Tree
- Watching out for the Wildlife
- Some Guideposts along the Path

9 You Can See the Forest for the Trees

By now you are well acquainted with the use of directories. Directories serve as a quick reference index to the contents of each floppy diskette. When listed with the DIR command, directories give the names and sizes of files and a date-time reference indicating when they were created or last modified.

Directories, of course, are not unique to the computer world. The most frequently used directory in the world is the phone book. The phone book is a simple directory. The listings are alphabetized by last name. An entry is listed in one location only, according to surname. When you know exactly the name you are looking for, the correct spelling, the first name initial or name *and* the address, you can find a number quickly.

But the phone directory also illustrates a problem with simple directories. When you have too much information, as when there are pages and pages of the same last name and that's all the information you have, they lose their effectiveness. Instead of being a helpful shortcut to information, they become a cumbersome burden.

This same situation can occur in your information retrieval system. When you accumulate too many files, you may actually dread the output of the DIR command. A double-sided diskette can hold up to 112 files, and listing the directory can involve several screens. Each screen must be stopped from scrolling and examined. This can take lots of time and cause grown computer users to cry.

Directly on the Path in Front of You

The difficulty of accessing and storing many files demanded a solution in two different areas. First, a new tool was needed that could store more files in less space. Actually, this tool, the *hard* or *fixed disk,* was borrowed from larger mainframe computer systems, which have always had a great deal of information to process. Now, 10-megabyte fixed disks are available for personal computers. A 10-megabyte fixed disk stores approximately 10 million characters. As you can imagine, that is either one incredibly long super-file, which might be impossible to use, or several hundred smaller files. A typical number of files on a hard disk might be anywhere from 500 to 800. Can you imagine using a DIR command and sitting through the listing? To say nothing of thinking up 798 unique file-names.

Obviously, the hard disk necessitated a new method of directory structuring. MS-DOS, again borrowing from mainframe computers and minicomputers, has provided the answer with the use of *tree-structured directories.*

In this type of structure, a main or *root* directory branches into several subdirectories, which in turn can generate other subdirectories. To move around from root to subdirectory or from subdirectory to subdirectory, you use a *path* that is included in a command as a *pathname.*

The use of tree-structured directories is designed to help you create order out of the confusion of many, many files. But their use is not limited to the larger capacity of fixed disk systems. You can use this structure on your floppy disk systems as well.

Since most of you probably haven't acquired a fixed disk yet, this discussion centers on the use of tree-structured directories for floppy disk users. If you do have a fixed disk system, this discussion as well as Chapter 11 will be of interest.

To illustrate the use of directories you are again going to take on a challenging role. In this chapter you are going to assume the alter ego of an agriculturalist who is using her new computer to organize the files in her growing business. To travel along your soon-to-be-created path, you will need an example diskette.

Preparing this diskette is going to do two useful things for you. First, it will show you just how much you have learned. These instructions, which would have seemed like Greek to you just a few short chapters ago, will now seem very easy to follow. Second, it will provide you with the necessary provisions to venture down the path to greater directory control.

You will need your system diskette to format a new diskette in this example. In addition, you will be copying an external command, TREE.COM, off the system diskette. Be sure your system diskette contains this file. To create the files on your example diskette, use the COPY CON method described in Chapter 8. Enter the commands listed on the left. Instructions and explanations are in the right hand column.

	Put your system diskette in drive A and a new diskette in drive B.
`A>format b:/s <ENTER>`	Format the diskette (include the system). When "Format another (Y/N)?" appears, press n.
`A>copy tree.com b: <ENTER>` `  1 File(s) copied`	This is a command file you'll need on the diskette.
`A>b: <ENTER>`	Change the current drive to B.
`B>copy con: weather <ENTER>`	Now we are going to create some "dummy" files. You can use EDLIN instead of COPY CON if you prefer.

`File contains weather information. <ENTER>`
`^Z <ENTER>`
`  1 File(s) copied`
	The contents of the files do not matter. We are making them short and to the point.

```
B>copy con: soil <ENTER>
File contains soil information. <ENTER>
^Z <ENTER>
   1 File(s) copied

B>copy con: yields <ENTER>
Record of last year's yields. <ENTER>
^Z <ENTER>
   1 File(s) copied

B>copy con: texture <ENTER>
Notes on fruit texture. <ENTER>
^Z <ENTER>
   1 File(s) copied

B>copy con: color <ENTER>
Notes on fruit color. <ENTER>
^Z <ENTER>
   1 File(s) copied
```

That's all there is to it. Five files created, just like that. You can take a look at your example diskette with DIR:

```
B>dir <ENTER>

   Volume in drive B has no label
   Directory of B:\

COMMAND   COM    17664 3-08-83      12:00P
TREE      COM     1513 3-08-83      12:00P
WEATHER             36 12-17-84      1:04P
SOIL                33 12-17-84      1:04P
YIELDS              31 12-17-84      1:05P
TEXTURE             25 12-17-84      1:05P
COLOR               23 12-17-84      1:06P
        7 File(s)    314368 bytes free
```

Everything all set? Let's begin blazing a path.

Getting to the Root of the Matter

Creating a root directory is easy. You have done it many times already. You see, FORMAT automatically creates a root directory *every time it formats a diskette*. The directory, which can hold up to 112 files, is the root directory of the tree-structured system. In MS-DOS version 2.0 and all later versions, this root directory can also hold subdirectories.

Subdirectories hold files. These files may contain groups of related data, or they may contain other subdirectories. MS-DOS treats all files the same. The only difference is that you can use subdirectories to get to other subdirectories. Once you are in a file, however, all you can do is go back to a directory. Sound a bit confusing?

Think about the maps you use when you go into the forest. These maps contain a maze of trails. Suppose a group of hikers starts out from the same point. This starting point, the "straight and narrow" trail, is like the root directory. It is the source of all other paths.

Some hikers follow the "straight and narrow" to "dead end" or "direct." These are their final destinations. Like a root directory, "straight and narrow" contains final destinations (locations where files are stored).

For other hikers, the "straight and narrow" is just the first step on a journey to "boomerang" or "over the hill." In this case, the root is the path to other subdirectories. The subdirectories "boomerang" and "over the hill" may contain final destinations of their own, where files are stored, or they may be links to other subdirectories such as "far away" and "diversion."

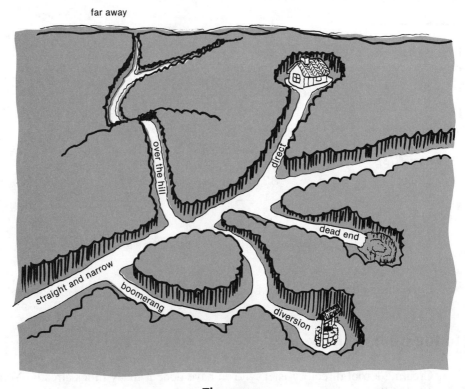

The map.

The important thing to realize about directories and subdirectories is that they contain files. Any of these files (locations) can also be subdirectories, paths to other files.

Subdirectories and Pathnames

The only function of a subdirectory is to group files. Like filenames, subdirectories may contain up to eight characters plus an optional three character extension. Each subdirectory must have a unique name and it cannot be a name of a file already contained in the root directory. Subdirectory names follow all the other rules for filenames.

Naming Subdirectories

Up to eight characters plus optional three character extension.

Each subdirectory must have a unique name.

Subdirectories cannot have the same name as a file already on the diskette.

Names must be valid characters for filenames and follow all other filenaming rules.

You find your way around in the directory by specifying a *pathname*. This is simply a list of names that tells MS-DOS where to start and which subdirectories to use to get to a final destination. Each subdirectory is separated from the next with a backslash (\). In your hiking adventure with the illustrated map, the following would be the path to the "edge of the forest:"

\boomerang\diversion\edge of the forest

You will notice that we did not mention the root directory, "straight and narrow," in this pathname. That is because the root directory is indicated by the initial backslash in the pathname. You never actually enter the directory name root, instead you use an initial backslash as a shorthand for this directory.

As a budding young agriculturist you are anxious to begin organizing your files. Your files are now on a diskette (the one you created earlier) and they are stored in the root directory. Files are always stored in the root directory until you tell MS-DOS to put them somewhere else. First, you are going to create a subdirectory called FRUITS. Within FRUITS you are going to have a subdirectory called CHERRIES. The CHERRIES subdirectory will contain a file named "yields". How do you clear a path to this file? First you tell MS-DOS where to start and then you give clear directions:

ROOT→ FRUITS → CHERRIES → YIELDS

```
\fruits\cherries\yields
```

This path translates into: starting from the root (indicated by the initial backslash), go to the file FRUITS (which is a subdirectory), go to the file CHERRIES (which is a subdirectory), and then find the file "yields". Don't worry *how* MS-DOS knows these are subdirectories; you'll find that out later in the chapter.

Almost all the commands in MS-DOS can be performed on specific files in different subdirectories. All you need to do is to tell MS-DOS which *path* to take to get to the file.

Pathnames are the secret organizing tools for sophisticated use of your disks. Subdirectories can save you lots of time and help you keep your files better organized. Pathnames are a quick way to create, copy, delete, and reorganize files. But don't get carried away. The best tree-structured directory is one that is simple.

If you make your structure too complicated, not only will you get lost on the path, MS-DOS will spend a lot of time simply arriving at the specified destination. One good idea, until you are more familiar with subdirectories and pathnames, is to limit your subdirectories to the root file. That way you will not stray too far off the beaten path.

Special Pathmarkers

There are some special commands MS-DOS reserves for creating and maintaining tree-structured directories—MKDIR, CHDIR, RMDIR, TREE, and PATH. Let's look at each of these commands in turn.

Be sure the diskette you are using with these examples is in drive A. For safety's sake, remove any diskette in drive B.

The MKDIR Command

use: creates a subdirectory

example: mkdir \fruits

abbreviation: md

When you FORMAT a diskette it contains one directory, the original root directory. To create subdirectories on the disk use the MKDIR (MaKe DIRectory)

command. Let's use MKDIR to create the subdirectory FRUITS. When using this command you may enter MKDIR or the shorter abbreviation MD. Put your example diskette in drive A.

MKDIR is an internal command. This means you can create a new directory whenever you are operating in MS-DOS (A or B prompt). This directory is being created from the root directory. Type in the command, followed by the symbol for the root (\) and then the subdirectory name:

```
A>mkdir \fruits <ENTER>
```

The computer makes those whirring sounds familiar to you from using the FORMAT and COPY commands. Then the MS-DOS prompt reappears. That's it, your new subdirectory now exists in the root directory on the diskette in the current drive.

Seem a bit too simple? Well, for you skeptics there is an easy way to verify the creation of FRUITS; use DIR to list the contents of the root directory. Nothing special is needed to do this; it is the same old DIR command you have come to know and love:

```
A>dir <ENTER>

   Volume in drive A has no label
   Directory of A:\

COMMAND  COM     17664   3-08-83   12:00P
TREE     COM      1513   3-08-83   12:00P
WEATHER             36  11-21-84    2:19P
SOIL                33  11-21-84    2:20P
YIELDS              31  11-21-84    2:22P
TEXTURE             25  11-21-84    3:27P
COLOR               23  11-21-84    3:32P
FRUITS          <DIR>   11-21-84    3:45P
        8 File(s)    313344 bytes free
```

Right there at the bottom of the list is FRUITS. MS-DOS nicely reminds you that this is a subdirectory by including the <DIR> extension. You are also given the date and time of "germination." The second line of this listing (Directory of A:\) tells you by means of the backslash, which is the root symbol, that you are looking at the root directory of A.

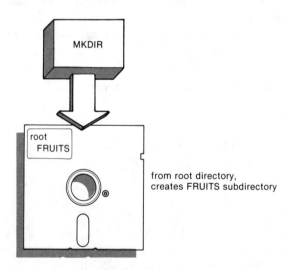

from root directory,
creates FRUITS subdirectory

The MKDIR Command.

Since you created this subdirectory from the root directory, you could have eliminated the first backslash. MS-DOS will always begin a directory operation from the directory you are in. In this case you are in root, so you don't need to include the initial \. The command could also look like this:

```
A>mkdir fruits
```

Suppose you wanted to do a lot of work with the FRUITS subdirectory. You were going to copy many files and perhaps create a few new subdirectories. Well, you can always get to a subdirectory by starting at the root and moving down one level with the pathname \FRUITS. But, just as you often change your current drive when you want to use drive B extensively, you can also *change your current directory*. This makes it easier to issue commands that refer only to a specified subdirectory.

The CHDIR Command

use: changes directories or identifies current directory

examples: chdir fruits
                    chdir \
                    chdir

abbreviation: cd

Changing directories is as easy as making them, simply give the CHDIR (CHange DIRectory) command. The command is followed by the name of the directory that you want as your base of operations. You may use the abbreviation CD if you wish. Since you are currently in the root directory, you don't need to include the opening \ in this command:

```
A>chdir fruits <ENTER>
```

This command instructs MS-DOS to change from the current directory to the subdirectory FRUITS. You will hear the disk drive whirring. And then there is silence. MS-DOS does not indicate that the directories have changed, it simply returns the A prompt. You can check which directory you are in by using DIR.

No beginning slash is necessary since you believe you are currently in the FRUITS subdirectory:

```
A>dir <ENTER>
```

What you are requesting is a directory listing of the *current directory*. Here is how MS-DOS responds:

```
Volume in drive A has no label
Directory of A:\fruits

   .          <DIR>      12-17-84      1:29P
   ..         <DIR>      12-17-84      1:29P
     2 File(s)      313344 bytes free
```
Your numbers may be different.

The second line of the directory message tells you what you want to know. It indicates this is a directory of the diskette in drive A:\fruits. Since the directory name is preceded by one slash, indicating the root directory, you know that this directory is a "first-level" subdirectory.

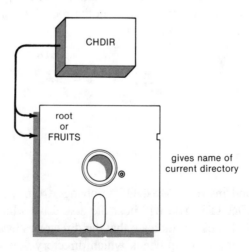

The CHDIR Command.

The next two lines of the directory listing are something you have not seen before. The single period and the double period stand for the directory itself and its "parent" directory. You'll explore these mysterious directory symbols a bit later.

The final line of the directory listing puts you back on familiar turf. It says there are two files in this directory, and gives the amount of bytes still available on the diskette.

While you are in this directory, you can do all the normal file operations *as long as the files exist in this directory*. If you try to do something with files in the root directory or in another subdirectory, you will be out on a limb. MS-DOS reminds you of your predicament with a "File not found" error message.

You are currently stuck in this subdirectory. You must issue another CHDIR command to get out of the subdirectory.

Getting Back to Your Roots

There is a quick and easy way to get back to the root directory no matter where you are within the subdirectory structure. You simply issue the CHDIR command with the root symbol, the single backslash (\):

```
A>chdir \ <ENTER>
```

Quicker than a summer downpour, you are home again. Use DIR to verify this:

```
A>dir <ENTER>

    Volume in drive A has no label
    Directory of A:\

COMMAND  COM    17664     3-08-83    12:00P
TREE     COM     1513     3-08-83    12:00P
WEATHER            36    11-21-84     2:19P
COIL               22    11-21-84     0:00P
YIELDS             31    11-21-84     2:22P
TEXTURE            25    11-21-84     3:27P
```

217

```
COLOR               23  11-21-84    3:32P
FRUITS          <DIR>     11-21-84    3:45P
          8 File(s)    313344 bytes free
```

You can tell you are in the root directory by the second line of the display, the directory message with a single backslash. Of course, you probably know that you are in the root because of the files listed. But when you have lots of files, and lots of diskettes, this second line will become very handy in identifying your current directory.

Keeping Current

There is another factor to keep in mind about current directories. Each drive you are using has its own separate current directory. For instance, you may have the example diskette in drive A. In drive B you have other data and program files. MS-DOS keeps track of a *separate current directory for each drive*. This can cause some confusion when you want to perform operations from one drive to another.

Suppose you want to copy the file "yields" into the root directory on the diskette in drive B. When you last worked on drive B you were using a word-processing program, which is contained under its own subdirectory, WP.

This is how MS-DOS views the current directories:

in drive A   the root directory of the example diskette
in drive B   the WP subdirectory

If you issue this copy command:

```
A>copy yields b:
```

MS-DOS would comply with your wishes. However, since the current directory on drive B is WP, that is the directory to which it would copy the file. You can see how this might confuse you when you went searching for "yields" in the root on B. (It is very simple to get the file to the right directory, but you must be sure to include the correct path.) For safety's sake, it is always a good idea to check on your current directories before you perform any operation.

To find out the current directory, just enter CHDIR by itself:

```
A>chdir <ENTER>
```

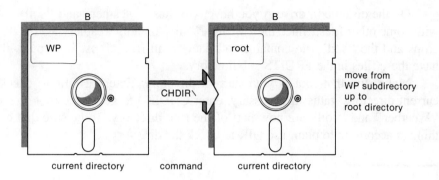

current directory   command   current directory

Current directory.

In this case, the change directory command really becomes the check (or identify) the current directory command. If you were in the root directory, you see this listing:

```
A:\
```

If you were in a subdirectory, the current directory would look like this:

```
A:\fruits
```

You can see that CHDIR is a versatile command, and also one that you will use a great deal. It allows you to change directories easily and quickly return to the root directory, and it provides quick identification of the current directory.

Finding the Right Home for a File

When you listed the contents of the FRUITS subdirectory, you noticed that the directory listed only the mysterious "." and ".." files; the rest of the subdirectory was empty. How do you get files into a subdirectory? The same way you always move files, with the COPY command.

On the diskette in drive A you have two files, "weather" and "soil", along with some other files. Since the "weather" file contains weather data on all fruit crops and the "soil" file contains soil data on all fruit crops, we would like to have these files in the FRUITS subdirectory.

Make sure that root is your current directory. Enter CHDIR to check the current directory status; if necessary, enter CHDIR \ to get to the root directory. "Weather" and "soil" are now part of the root directory. To be sure that everything is according to plan, use DIR to check the directory:

```
A>dir <ENTER>

    Volume in drive A has no label
    Directory of A:\

COMMAND  COM      17664    3-08-83   12:00P
TREE     COM       1513    3-08-83   12:00P
WEATHER             36    11-21-84    2:19P
SOIL                33    11-21-84    2:20P
YIELDS              31    11-21-84    2:22P
TEXTURE             25    11-21-84    3:27P
COLOR               23    11-21-84    3:32P
FRUITS        <DIR>       11-21-84    3:45P
        8 File(s)      313344 bytes free
```

Since this is the same procedure you use to copy files from one diskette to another, think of the transfer in terms of source and target. The directory which currently holds the files is the source directory. The subdirectory to which the files will be copied is the target directory. To MS-DOS, FRUITS is just like any other file. As long as you specify a source and a target, it will copy the files, even if one of those files happens to be a subdirectory:

```
A>copy weather fruits <ENTER>
        1 File(s) copied

A>copy soil fruits <ENTER>
        1 File(s) copied
```

That's all. As easy as that you have two new files in your FRUITS subdirectory. The files have not been deleted from the root directory; they have simply been duplicated in the FRUITS subdirectory. You can check this by using DIR. First make sure the files are still in the root directory. Since this is your current directory, just enter DIR:

```
A>dir <ENTER>

    Volume in drive A has no label
    Directory of A:\

COMMAND   COM    17664    3-08-83   12:00P
TREE      COM     1513    8-30-84   12:00P
WEATHER            36    12-17-84    1:04P
SOIL               33    12-17-84    1:04P
YIELDS             31    12-17-84    1:05P
TEXTURE            25    12-17-84    1:05P
COLOR              23    12-17-84    1:06P
FRUITS         <DIR>     12-17-84    1:29P
        8 File(s)    311296 bytes free
```

You can see that both "weather" and "soil" are still in this directory.

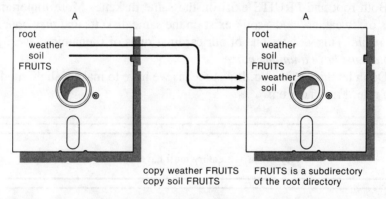

copy weather FRUITS   FRUITS is a subdirectory
copy soil FRUITS   of the root directory

Copying files to a subdirectory.

One way to verify that "weather" and "soil" are also part of the FRUITS subdirectory is to change the current directory to FRUITS and then use the DIR command:

```
A>chdir fruits <ENTER>
A>dir <ENTER>
```

But you can also check on FRUITS without leaving the root directory, that is, without changing the current directory. Just ask for a directory listing with a pathname:

```
A>dir \fruits <ENTER>

    Volume in drive A has no label
    Directory of A:\fruits

.            <DIR>        12-17-84    1:29P
..           <DIR>        12-17-84    1:29P
WEATHER             36    12-17-84    1:04P
SOIL                33    12-17-84    1:04P
        4 File(s)   311296 bytes free
```

You can see that the two files have now been added to the directory of the FRUITS subdirectory. A comparison of the amount of bytes still free will show you that the space on the diskette has been reduced by the number of bytes in these two files.

Both root and FRUITS exist on the same diskette. More importantly, two copies of "weather" and "soil" exist on the same diskette and *they both have the same name*. This violates one of our cardinal rules of filenaming: *every file on a diskette must have a unique name*.

Don't let this shake you. It just means we have to make a slight modification of the rule. From now on:

> Every file in a directory must have a unique name.

While this capability of having duplicate files may seem confusing at first, it also has many advantages. With tree-structured directories, you cannot perform an operation on a file unless it is located in the subdirectory in which you are working. So sometimes, if files are not very long, it is convenient to have duplicates of certain files in a subdirectory.

For instance, if you were going to do some word processing on specific files, it would be necessary to have these files in the same subdirectory as your word-processing program. (Later we will give you some hints that will help you minimize the need for duplicate files, but for now let's carry on with the example.)

You are now ready to create a new subdirectory on this diskette. Not only do you grow fruits, but you also have extensive lumber holdings. So your new subdirectory is named LUMBER. It so happens that your "weather" and "soil" files also contain information on conditions related to effective forest management. So you want these files in this new subdirectory also. If you are still in the

\FRUITS directory change back to root with CHDIR \. Starting in the root directory, you can perform this operation with three simple commands:

```
A>mkdir lumber <ENTER>

A>copy weather lumber <ENTER>
        1 File(s) copied

A>copy soil lumber <ENTER>
        1 File(s) copied
```

To check on the creation of this subdirectory, first ask for a directory of root, your current directory:

```
A>dir <ENTER>

    Volume in drive A has no label
    Directory of A:\

COMMAND COM    17664    3-08-83    12:00P
TREE    COM     1513    3-08-83    12:00P
WEATHER           36   12-17-84     1:04P
SOIL              33   12-17-84     1:04P
YIELDS            31   12-17-84     1:05P
TEXTURE           25   12-17-84     1:05P
COLOR             23   12-17-84     1:06P
FRUITS        <DIR>    12-17-84     1:29P
LUMBER        <DIR>    12-17-84     1:42P
        9 File(s)    308224 bytes free
```

Yes, the new subdirectory LUMBER is part of your root directory.

Now let's make sure that our two files have been copied to the new subdirectory:

```
A>dir \lumber <ENTER>

    Volume in drive A has no label
    Directory of A:\lumber

.              <DIR>    12-17-84     1:42P
..             <DIR>    12-17-84     1:42P
```

```
WEATHER         36   12-17-84   1:04P
SOIL            33   12-17-84   1:04P
        4 File(s)    308224 bytes free
```

And that's it. Now you are proficient not only at creating new directories, but at modifying their contents to fit your needs.

Blazing New Trails

Your tree-structured directory now has two levels. The home base is the parent or root directory. This is level 0 or the starting point. Beneath this level there are two first-level subdirectories, FRUIT and LUMBER. But what about the files contained in these directories? How do we get to a specific file within a specific subdirectory?

To find a file, MS-DOS must have two pieces of information, the name of the file and the name of the directory that contains that file. And since subdirectories can contain other subdirectories, you need to specify the exact path that leads to the file you want.

You can get to a file in two different ways. The first is to start in the root directory and then list all of the subdirectories that intervene between the root and the directory holding the file. The second is to change to the desired subdirectory with CHDIR and then call the file.

Alternative paths

To find and list a file in a subdirectory from the root directory:

- Ask for it by name—
  TYPE fruits\weather

- Change the directory—
  chdir\fruits
  and ask for the file—
  TYPE weather

Suppose you want a listing of a file in the FRUITS directory called "weather". You are now in the root directory. Ask for the listing using the correct pathname:

```
A>type fruits\weather <ENTER>
```

Or use CHDIR to change the current directory:

```
A>chdir fruits <ENTER>
```

and then use the TYPE command:

```
A>type weather <ENTER>
```

Your FRUITS subdirectory contains files that pertain to all your fruit crops. But now you want to create another subdirectory within FRUITS to be named CHERRIES. CHERRIES will be a second-level subdirectory; that is, two levels down from the root directory. Get back to the root directory by using CHDIR \ (you might still be in LUMBER). To create subdirectories in subdirectories you use the MKDIR (or simply MD) command:

```
A>md \fruits\cherries <ENTER>
```

In this pathname you specified two directory names, the subdirectory which already exists and the new subdirectory you are creating. All directories must be separated by slashes. The actual message received by MS-DOS from this command translates like this: *"Starting from the root directory (indicated by the initial backslash), go down to the first-level subdirectory FRUITS, and create a new second-level subdirectory named CHERRIES.*

As usual, MS-DOS does not inform you that the directory was created, it simply returns to the prompt. You can confirm that this subdirectory now exists *directly from your current position in the root directory:*

```
A>dir fruits <ENTER>
```

Here is how the display looks:

```
    Volume in drive A has no label
    Directory of A:\fruits

.              <DIR>        12-17-84      1:29P
..             <DIR>        12-17-84      1:29P
WEATHER               36    12-17-84      1:04P
SOIL                  33    12-17-84      1:04P
CHERRIES       <DIR>        12-17-84      1:45P
        5 file(s)       307200 bytes free
```

You can see that the CHERRIES subdirectory is now part of FRUITS.

If you want to check on the contents of CHERRIES, you must give the correct path:

```
A>dir \fruits\cherries <ENTER>
```

The first backslash tells MS-DOS that FRUITS is a subdirectory of root; the next slash indicates that CHERRIES is a subdirectory of FRUITS. If you wish, you can eliminate the first slash because root is your current directory and MS-

DOS always begins its search with the current directory. Here is the listing for the previous command:

```
        Volume in drive A has no label
        Directory of A:\fruits\cherries

  .        <DIR>     12-17-84    1:45P
  ..       <DIR>     12-17-84    1:45P
   2 File(s)    307200 bytes free
```

The second line in the listing confirms that this is a second-level directory, a subdirectory of a subdirectory. So our entire directory structure now looks like this:

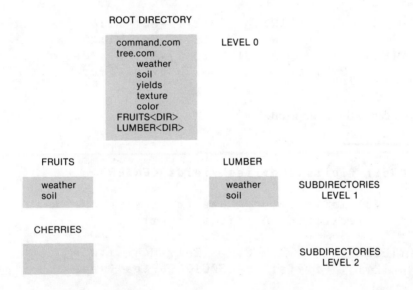

Of course, the subdirectories can contain many other files, but for simplicity we will mention only the ones we are using in our examples.

The Path of Least Resistance

Almost any MS-DOS command can be used on any file in a subdirectory. The only secret is to establish the correct path to the file.

The CHERRIES subdirectory in our FRUITS subdirectory is currently empty. Let's copy the "yields" file, currently in the root directory, into this new subdirectory. Make sure root is your current directory before attempting this.

```
A>copy yields fruits\cherries <ENTER>
```

If you want, check the contents of this subdirectory with DIR:

```
A>dir fruits\cherries <ENTER>

    Volume in drive A has no label
    Directory of A:\fruits\cherries

  .              <DIR>        12-17-84    1:45P
  ..             <DIR>        12-17-84    1:45P
YIELDS              31        12-17-84    1:05P
        3 File(s)       306176 bytes free
```

Or you can call the file itself:

```
A>dir fruits\cherries\yields <ENTER>

    Volume in drive A has no label
    Directory of A:\fruits\cherries

YIELDS              31        12-17-84    1:05P
        1 File(s)       306176 bytes free
```

When you are tracing a path to a file, first list the intervening subdirectories (separated by slashes). The filename comes last.

This illustrates how you move down through a directory. But you can also move up in the tree structure. To move up one level, just change the directory to the "parent" directory:

```
A>cd fruits\cherries <ENTER>
```

Your current directory is now the subdirectory CHERRIES. Use DIR to be sure you are in the correct subdirectory.

```
A>dir <ENTER>

    Volume in drive A has no label
    Directory of A:\fruits\cherries

.               <DIR>       12-17-84    1:45P
..              <DIR>       12-17-84    1:45P
YIELDS              31      12-17-84    1:05P
        3 File(s)      306176 bytes free
```

Taking a Shortcut

Now you are finally going to find out the meaning of those curious directory entries "." (period) and ".." (double period).

In the previous example, you moved up in the directory structure by using the CHDIR command and listing the name of the "parent" directory. This is a valid way to move up in a directory. But MS-DOS has given us a shortcut to move up one level, but still not affect the current directory.

Be sure your current directory is still CHERRIES. Now enter this command:

```
A>dir .. <ENTER>    Leave a space between dir and the periods.
```

You will see this display:

```
    Volume in drive A has no label
    Directory of A:\fruits

.               <DIR>       12-17-84    1:29P
..              <DIR>       12-17-84    1:29P
WEATHER             36      12-17-84    1:04P
SOIL                31      12-17-84    1:04P
CHERRIES        <DIR>       12-17-84    1:45P
        5 File(s)      306176 bytes free
```

How did you get back to FRUITS? What happened is that you have moved up one level.

This double period symbol tells MS-DOS: *"Move me to the current directory's parent directory."* As long as you are not in the root directory, you can use this "*..*" convention to move one level up *without* specifying the directory's name. *This does not affect the status of your current directory.*

Now issue the DIR command with a single period:

```
A>dir . <ENTER>   Leave a space between dir and the period.


    Volume in drive A has no label
    Directory of A:\fruits\cherries

.              <DIR>      12-17-84    1:45P
..             <DIR>      12-17-84    1:45P
YIELDS             31    12-17-84    1:05P
        3 File(s)     306176 bytes free
```

The CHERRIES subdirectory is listed. The single period tells MS-DOS: *"Apply this command to me, the current directory."* Notice that using the period conventions *does not change the current directory.*

"." and ".."

These symbols:	tell MS-DOS to apply this command to:
..	my parent directory
.	me, the current directory

The single and double period conventions are only used in subdirectories. They do not appear in root directories.

You don't have to use these symbols, and don't do so at first if they confuse you. But gradually, as you become more familiar with tree-structured directories, try experimenting with their use again. They may save you a lot of time.

Climbing around in the Tree

To really understand the usefulness of the tree-structured directory system, you need to practice a bit with moving around in the structure. To do this we are going to use the COPY command.

First, let's add a little complexity to our tree. You now want to enter your records on a second crop, peaches. The logical place for this new data seems to be a subdirectory under FRUITS. Move back to the root directory using CHDIR \ (assuming you are still in the FRUITS\CHERRIES subdirectory):

```
A>mkdir \fruits\peaches <ENTER>
```

The information that you want to store in this subdirectory is in the file "color" ("color" is currently in the root directory):

```
A>copy color fruits\peaches <ENTER>
```

The system replies:

```
1 File(s) copied
```

But to illustrate a point, let's assume that the file you want to include in this directory is on another diskette. Then the command would look like this:

```
A>copy b:color fruits\peaches <ENTER>
```

MS-DOS allows you to copy information from a file on one diskette to a directory or subdirectory on a diskette in another drive. All you need to do is include the drive indicator.

There is one more file in the root directory that you want to include in this PEACHES subdirectory. It is called "texture".

```
A>copy texture fruits\peaches <ENTER>
```

If you want to, use the DIR command now to verify the new subdirectory and its contents:

```
A>dir fruits\peaches <ENTER>

    Volume in drive A had no label
    Directory of A:\fruits\peaches

 .             <DIR>       12-17-84    1:53P
 ..            <DIR>       12-17-84    1:53P
COLOR                23   12-17-84    1:06P
TEXTURE              25   12-17-84    1:05P
        4 File(s)     303104 bytes free
```

As a final step, we are going to create a new subdirectory in LUMBER. This is called REDWOOD:

```
A>mkdir lumber\redwood <ENTER>
```

As can happen with tree-structured directories, you may be feeling a bit lost right now. So, for your convenience, here is a map of our current, complete, tree-structured directory:

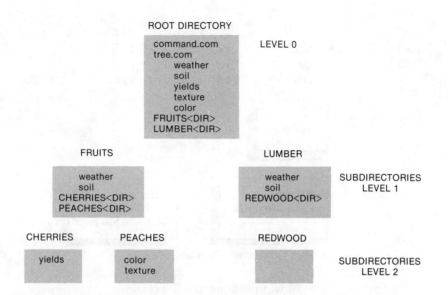

The purpose of all this intrigue is to show you how to get information from one subdirectory to another.

Within the CHERRIES subdirectory is a file called "yields". You have spent a lot of time setting up this file and now want to use the same general contents in your REDWOOD subdirectory. Here are the steps you take to transfer "yields" from one subdirectory to another.

First, make sure you are in the root directory. Since you are dealing with second-level directories, you must go up to the root and then down into the subdirectories. You can't go across to level one or level two subdirectories; the path must go through the common link, the root:

```
A>copy fruits\cherries\yields lumber\redwood<ENTER>
      1 File(s) copied
```

A DIR command confirms the copy:

```
A>dir lumber\redwood <ENTER>

    Volume in drive A has no label
    Directory of A:\lumber\redwood
```

```
    .            <DIR>      12-17-84    1:56P
    ..           <DIR>      12-17-84    1:56P
 YIELDS             31      12-17-84    1:05P
    3 File(s)      301056 bytes  free
```

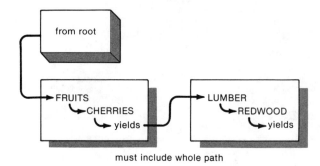

must include whole path

Moving around subdirectories.

So here is the advantage of tree-structured directories. You can move quickly within a complex structure. This can be essential when you are dealing with a large number of files on a fixed disk. But this COPY command also demonstrates the importance of clear, easily defined paths. You can see that if you create too many subdirectories within subdirectories, you can easily get lost in the resulting forest. A friendly reminder once again, keep the paths simple.

Watching out for the Wildlife

All of the normal rules associated with the COPY command are in effect when you are working with subdirectories. Suppose, for instance, that you want to copy the contents of the subdirectory PEACHES into REDWOOD. You want to copy *all* the files in the subdirectory, so the easiest method is to use a wildcard with the COPY command. PEACHES contains two files, "color" and "texture". (Why you would want these files in LUMBER/REDWOOD is a discussion best left to the farmer and his forest supervisor!) Using the wildcard you would issue this command:

```
A>copy \fruits\peaches\*.* \lumber\redwood <ENTER>
```

MS-DOS will tell you what is going on:

```
A:\FRUITS\PEACHES\COLOR
A:\FRUITS\PEACHES\TEXTURE
       2 Files(s) copied
```

Both files in PEACHES are now also in REDWOOD.

The usual caution when using wildcards apply. Make sure you want all the files, or a number of files that are similar, to be copied before becoming involved with wildcards.

Now check the contents of LUMBER\REDWOOD with the DIR command:

```
A>dir \lumber\redwood <ENTER>

    Volume in drive A has no label
    Directory of A:\lumber\redwood

 .                <DIR>       12-17-84    1:56P
 ..               <DIR>       12-17-84    1:56P
 YIELDS              31       12-17-84    1:05P
 COLOR               23       12-17-84    1:06P
 TEXTURE             25       12-17-84    1:05P
        5 File(s)       299008 bytes free
```

After you have worked hard and long to build a beautiful, well-designed, tree-structured directory, you have reason to be proud. But like all things, this structure cannot last forever. As your computing needs expand and change, you will need to keep your directories up-to-date. And eventually you will find that some of them are, sadly, obsolete or pretty useless. If you just go on building bigger and better directories, you will make path finding both confusing and time consuming.

Well, just as MS-DOS provides DEL (or ERASE) to eliminate no-longer-needed files, it also presents a command to rid you of unnecessary directories.

The RMDIR Command

use: removes directories

example: rmdir peaches

abbreviation: rd

The RMDIR (ReMove DIRectory) command helps you with the housekeeping chores in your directory structure. But before you can eliminate a directory you must first provide for the files inside it. This is a safety feature that MS-DOS builds into the directory structure. It can save you from accidentally erasing a file you want while eliminating a directory.

Suppose that halfway through the growing season there is a terrible infestation of Tasmanian peach flies. Your entire peach crop is down the drain and you destroy all your peach trees. Well, you certainly don't need your PEACHES subdirectory cluttering up your directory structure. In fact, even the sight of the name reduces you to tears.

To remove this directory you must first get to the correct subdirectory:

```
A>chdir fruits\peaches <ENTER>

A>dir <ENTER>                        As with all erase functions, be
                                     careful! Be sure you are in the
                                     correct subdirectory.
```

```
      Volume in drive A has no label
      Directory of A:\fruits\peaches

.             <DIR>        12-17-84    1:53P
..            <DIR>        12-17-84    1:53P
COLOR                 23   12-17-84    1:06P
TEXTURE               25   12-17-84    1:05P
        4 File(s)     299008 bytes free
```

Now erase the files in the subdirectory:

```
A>erase *.* <ENTER>                  Be sure you don't need any of
                                     the files before you erase!
Are you sure (Y/N)? y <ENTER>        You answer yes.
```

With the files gone, you can erase the subdirectory. You must be "one level up" from the subdirectory you want to erase.

```
A>cd .. <ENTER>              Move up to the FRUITS subdirectory.

A>rmdir peaches <ENTER>      Now remove the subdirectory.
```

Using RMDIR

First, eliminate all files in the subdirectory: erase *.*

Second, go up to the parent directory: chdir ..

Third, use rmdir to remove the directory: rmdir (directory name)

It is a good idea to use DIR to be sure the subdirectory is gone:

```
A>dir <ENTER>

    Volume in drive A has no label
    Directory of A:\fruits

 .              <DIR>         12-17-84      1:29P
 ..             <DIR>         12-17-84      1:29P
WEATHER               36      12-17-84      1:04P
SOIL                  33      12-17-84      1:04P
CHERRIES        <DIR>         12-17-84      1:45P
        5 File(s)     302080 bytes free
```

Good bye peaches, better luck next year!

When you modify your tree structure frequently, it is often difficult to keep track of exactly which files and subdirectories belong where. How can you quickly get an overview of the tree structure on any given diskette?

Well, one way is to use DIR and note all the files with the <DIR> extension. Then you can use CHDIR to reach each of these subdirectories, and DIR again, while noting which files are <DIR> files here and so on. This is time-consuming and rather frustrating. Once again, MS-DOS has anticipated this need and provides a command to give you a handy pocket guide to your overall directory.

The TREE Command

use: displays every pathname on a given diskette

switches: /f   lists the files in each subdirectory

example: tree a:

TREE is an external command, so to use it you must have your system diskette in drive A or a copy of TREE.COM on the diskette you want to examine. And, of course, you must be in the directory that holds that command. Make sure you are in the root directory and issue this command. Include the /f switch to get a listing of files in each subdirectory:

```
A>tree /f <ENTER>
```

Here is the TREE display for our example diskette:

```
DIRECTORY PATH LISTING FOR VOLUME ??????????

Path: \FRUITS

Sub-directories:   CHERRIES

Files:             WEATHER
                   SOIL


Path: \FRUITS\CHERRIES

Sub-directories:   None

Files:             YIELDS


Path: \LUMBER

Sub-directories:   REDWOOD

Files:             WEATHER
                   SOIL


Path: \LUMBER\REDWOOD

Sub-directories:   None

Files:             YIELDS
                   COLOR
                   TEXTURE
```

When you call for a file, MS-DOS looks for it only in the current directory. If you specify a pathname, then MS-DOS looks there. It looks for the file in only one location. This is true whether you are using an MS-DOS command, such as COPY, or executing a program that needs a data file. Only one directory is searched, either the current one or the one specified in a path. This is also true of your program files. When you call for a program, MS-DOS immediately searches for it in the current directory. If it is not found, it won't be executed.

But programs have an extra advantage over other files in tree-structured directories. The search for programs can be extended to other directories by using a special command.

The PATH Command

use: defines a path to search for DOS commands, program files, or batch files not found in the current directory

example: path ACCTING;\PROGS\MISC;\

The PATH command does not have anything to do with the use of pathnames in general. It is only used to search for DOS commands, programs files, and batch files. The names in a PATH command must be separated by semicolons.

Since you don't have any program files or batch files in your directory, you will have to abandon the orchards for a moment and dwell in the land of pure fantasy. Imagine that you are in a subdirectory on drive A that is called \NEW-PROGS. You are looking for a program called RUNSUM.BAS. Here is how you tell MS-DOS where to look for the program.

```
A>path \ACCTING;\PROGS\MISC;\ <ENTER>
```

Then, when you enter the program name "RUNSUM.BAS", MS-DOS searches for the program in four places:

- the current directory (this is automatic)

- the ACCTING directory under the root

- the MISC directory under the PROGS directory under the root

- and, finally, the root itself (indicated by \)

The PATH command can also search in directories on other drives. Just include the drive designator in the PATH command:

```
A>path \ACCTING;\PROGS\MISC;B:\OLDPROGS <ENTER>
```

If you enter PATH without any other information, MS-DOS will search the last path it was given. To discontinue this extensive searching feature, enter PATH with a single semicolon:

```
A>path ; <ENTER>
```

After this command, the search reverts to the current directory only.

Some Guideposts along the Path

Like many tools in MS-DOS, tree-structured directories can be useful or they can be mystifying. The idea here is to start slowly and build as you go. As long as your directory structure makes sense to you and is logical for your needs, it will save you lots of time and energy.

But don't get carried away creating a new subdirectory for every file. Obviously, if your computer spends all its time tracing down subdirectories and files, you will never get anything else done. Every time MS-DOS establishes a subdirectory, it uses up approximately 500 additional bytes of RAM. If you create too many subdirectories, you may one day find that you don't have enough room to run large programs.

When creating directories, keep in mind the mechanics of moving around inside them. While it is easy to move up and down a limb, it is impossible, even if you were an orangutan, to swing between limbs. Make sure that your "levels" contain logical subdirectories, and that you eliminate the need to go up and down again to get to a file you use frequently.

On floppy disk systems it is a good idea to keep all your subdirectories in the root. This makes it easy for you to find exactly what you need without time-consuming searches.

If possible, keep data files that run with specific programs in the same directory. Then, when a program needs a data file, it can find it right in the current directory.

Keep all utilities and command files that you use a great deal in the root directory. This will save you time and make them available for all files in the directories under the root.

You can even keep most of your programs in the root directory. Once you have established a home for your programs, use PATH to keep these programs readily available.

Give you subdirectories distinct names. The confusion you save may be your own.

This concludes your entry into the complex, exciting world of tree-structured directories. Using this tool, with restraint, on floppy disk systems is a convenience. But using this tool on fixed disks is a necessity. In this chapter you have learned about root directories and subdirectories. You have traveled along the path to find better file organization. In addition to learning how to put files in a subdirectory, you have moved around inside the tree-structured directory to create pathnames to find and store your files. Finally, you have become familiar with the directory commands: MKDIR, CHDIR, RMDIR, TREE, and PATH.

Plumbing Techniques

10   Plumbing Techniques

The title of this chapter may sound to you like a text for a beginning plumbing class. You're probably wondering what it is doing as a chapter in a book on operating systems.

But hold on. The plumbing techniques we will discuss—pipes, filters, and redirection—are actually sophisticated data management commands. These commands give you choices in determining where your information comes from (input) and where it goes after you're finished with it (output). They are the frosting on the cake in allowing you to make the most of your MS-DOS operating system.

Diverting the Flow

You know from your own computer use that normally you enter information from your keyboard. The keyboard is the *standard information device* in personal computer systems.

When you want to look at your input or see the results of programs, you use your screen. The monitor or display screen is the *standard output device* in personal computer systems.

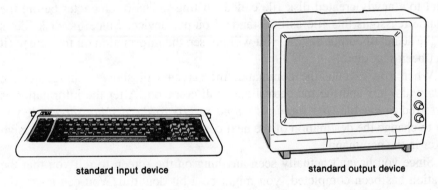

standard input device   standard output device

Keyboard and display.

However, it is possible, using MS-DOS version 2, to use other devices for input and output. For example, a file can be the source of input and a second file can be the location of the output.

DOS sees things in black and white. There is a standard input device and a standard output device. By default these are the keyboard and display screen. But DOS doesn't really care what provides the input and output *as long as you label them as the standard input and output devices* when issuing commands. When you designate files, programs, or other devices as the means of input and/or output, you are using the concept of *redirection*.

Redirecting Standard Output

The reasons why you might want to redirect output are numerous. Perhaps a specific program or command results in a new version of your data; you would like to keep this information in a separate file. Or you may want to have data automatically output to the printer. Perhaps you want to add output information to an already existing file.

No doubt you recognize this symbol ">" from your high school math classes. It means greater than. But in MS-DOS this symbol indicates the *redirection of output*. Think of it as standing for *send to this place,* with the arrow pointing the way to the file, program, or device to receive the information. Here is how you might redirect the output of a DIR command:

```
A>dir >listing <ENTER>
```

As a result of this command, the directory of the diskette in the current drive is sent to a newly created disk file called "listing". The > character before the filename reassigns this file as the standard output device. Since the disk file is now the standard output device, you will not see the information on the screen (it hasn't been sent there!).

When you execute the command, the screen will show nothing, but the drives will whirr and the indicator lights will come on. After the information is transferred to the file, *the standard output reverts to the display screen.* If you want to change the destination of the next command, you must include a reassign marker in the command.

Since you haven't actually seen anything on the screen to tell you that the operation has been completed, you might be a bit doubtful. You can check the new file by using the TYPE command:

```
A>type listing <ENTER>
```

The contents of the file "listing" will appear on the screen.

You can use directories and subdirectories in redirecting output. For example:

```
A>dir \fruits\cherries >fruitdir <ENTER>
```

This puts the directory listing of the \FRUITS\CHERRIES subdirectory into a file called "fruitdir".

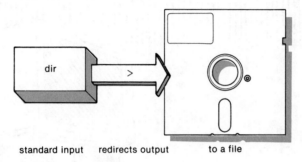

standard input   redirects output   to a file

Redirection of output.

One thing to keep in mind as you redirect output to files. If you redirect to an already existing file, the contents of the file are wiped out. But there is a simple solution to this problem: when you want to *append the new output to the end of an already existing file* you include >> in the command:

```
A>dir >>fruitdir <ENTER>
```

With this command, the directory listing of the current directory is put into the "fruitdir" file at the end of the contents of the file as it currently exists.

Redirection using >> is a handy way of keeping updated listings of your directories all in one file or for updating any information in a file (e.g., a mailing list). You're going to find this feature very "user friendly."

Redirecting Standard Input

As you might expect, the opposite of output redirection is *input redirection*. This operation is symbolized by the less than character, "<". Think of this symbol as saying *take the contents from this file and use it as input*. Using this option you can make the standard input device a file instead of the keyboard. The uses for input redirection are a bit more obscure than for output redirection. One very common use is to relieve yourself of the repetitious entries needed to start up a program. Simply include the responses necessary in a file named, for instance, "answers". Then redirect the input using this file.

But by far the most frequent use of redirected input is with the use of *filters* in *piping* information. Let's look at this piping feature.

The Trans-DOS Pipeline

Although there are no real pipes involved, the analogy of a pipeline is a useful tool for understanding the flow of information from input to output devices.

When a water department constructs a pipeline, they lay sections of pipe in a line to form one long conduit. The pipeline takes water from its source, and pipes it to a water storage area. Along the way, there are reservoirs which store the water temporarily. The water is then sent to a purification plant, where it is filtered before it is piped to its final destination, your home.

When you construct an MS-DOS pipeline, you do very much the same thing. The data you are going to put into the pipeline is stored in a source file or program. You want to use the output of this program or file as the input to the next program or command. In this way you can "hook" commands, programs, and files together, like sections of pipe, in a long chain.

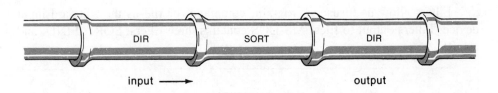

Piping.

The data, however, does not go directly from the input file to the output file. If it did, you could accomplish the same goal by simply copying the file. Instead, in piping, the data is fed in from the input file, goes through a "filtering" process where it is modified, and then goes to its destination in the output file.

When you use piping, it appears to MS-DOS that the input is the same as if it were typed in from the keyboard. But in reality, MS-DOS creates internal "temporary" files, like reservoirs, to hold the data as it is being piped. You will encounter some of these temporary files as you work your way through the examples in this chapter. Just so you have fair warning, they appear in your directory like this:

```
%PIPEx.$$$
```

where *x* is an integer to distinguish different PIPE files.

Does this *still* sound like an introductory class in plumbing? Let's see if we can make this concept as clear as a sparkling stream by diving further into filters.

Filtering the Flow

Filters are DOS commands or programs that read in data from the designated standard input device, modify the data in some way, and then output the modified data to the designated standard output device. Thus, by its position in the middle of the process, this command works to "filter" the data.

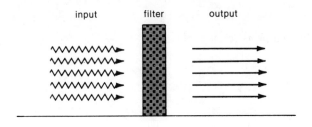

Filtering.

Filters allow us to use a program, command, or file as the standard input device. Filters output to files. MS-DOS contains three filters: SORT, FIND, and MORE.

The SORT Filter

use: sorts file contents either alphabetically or by column number

switches: /r   sort in reverse alphabetical order
               /+n   sort on the column indicated by n

examples: sort <b:wines
              sort/r <b:wines
              sort/+28 <b:wines
              sort/+50 <b:wines >country
              dir ¦ sort

Learning to use SORT is like learning how to drive. You know you existed without it, but it's hard to imagine how. That is a pretty strong statement, but I think you'll be enthusiastic too. But to experience the real pleasure of using SORT, you have to try it on some actual data. So we are going to create a file to play SORT with.

For our SORT adventure you will need a formatted diskette; if you can find it, use the diskette you formatted with the volume label "wine cellar" in the exercise in Chapter 7. If you can't find it, maybe you should review "The Ten Commandments of Disk Handling and Usage" in Chapter 4. In any case, if you don't have this diskette handy, just format another one:

```
A>format b:/v <ENTER>
```

When the volume name is requested enter:

```
wine cellar <ENTER>
```

Put your system diskette, which contains the filters in the SORT.EXE, FIND.EXE, and MORE.COM files, in drive A and your formatted diskette in drive B.

Now here are the rules for the SORT script. You are a connoisseur of fine wines and have a "respectable" wine cellar. But the only way to keep up with its contents is to immediately catalog all new purchases before you can taste any of them.

The first thing you need is a list of your new bottles of wine. Create a file called "wines" on the diskette in drive B. The name starts in column 1, the year in column 23, the appellation in column 28, and the country in column 50.

You must create this file as an ASCII text file (see Chapter 6). That means you should use EDLIN or COPY CON to enter the text. Also, do not use the <TAB> key to space between columns because SORT cannot handle this character. Okay, here are your latest finds:

```
A>copy con: b:wines <ENTER>

Lafite                  45 Bordeaux              France
Phelps Insignia         74 Cabernet Sauvignon    U.S.A.
Ridge Gyserville        73 Zinfandel             U.S.A.
La Mission Haut Brion   64 Bordeaux              France
Y'Quem                  58 Sauterne              France
^Z <ENTER>
```

You can use the TYPE command to check the contents of your list:

```
A>type b:wines <ENTER>
```

Is your mouth watering? Wait till you see what SORT can do with this list.

Now on your mark, get set, go.

The first thing you want is an alphabetical listing of the names of the new bottles to make it easier to enter them into your master file. This means that you want to SORT on the first column. (An alphabetical sort on the first column is the default condition of SORT.)

SORT accepts input from another program, command, or file. But you must include the reassignment character as part of the statement:

```
A>sort <b:wines <ENTER>
```

With this command you have told MS-DOS to sort the contents of the file "wines". Now watch the screen:

```
La Mission Haut Brion  64  Bordeaux             France
Lafite                 45  Bordeaux             France
Phelps Insignia        74  Cabernet Sauvignon  U.S.A.
Ridge Gyserville       73  Zinfandel           U.S.A.
Y'Quem                 58  Sauterne             France
```

Pretty fast and easy, huh?

SORT will also sort by reverse alphabetical order. I'm not sure why you would want to in this particular case, but it's best to know all your options.

To perform a sort so the end of the alphabet tops the list, you use the /r option:

```
A>sort/r <b:wines <ENTER>
```

And here it is!

```
Y'Quem                 58  Sauterne             France
Ridge Gyserville       73  Zinfandel           U.S.A.
Phelps Insignia        74  Cabernet Sauvignon  U.S.A.
Lafite                 45  Bordeaux             France
La Mission Haut Brion  64  Bordeaux             France
```

But SORT has even more surprises in store. Suppose you want to list your acquisitions by year, from the oldest to the newest. This helps in planning storage.

To do this you use the / + n option. This switch allows you to sort by any column (indicated by the *n* in the command). You want to sort by year, which begins in the 23d column, so enter this command:

```
A>sort/+23 <b:wines <ENTER>
```

Immediately you have your new listing:

```
Lafite                   45  Bordeaux              France
Y'Quem                   58  Sauterne              France
La Mission Haut Brion    64  Bordeaux              France
Ridge Gyserville         73  Zinfandel             U.S.A.
Phelps Insignia          74  Cabernet Sauvignon    U.S.A.
```

And there you go, from oldest to youngest.

You probably also have need of keeping a listing of your wines by appellation. That's the information that begins in column 28. Again, you use the / + n switch:

```
A>sort/+28 <b:wines <ENTER>
```

Voila!

```
Lafite                   45  Bordeaux              France
La Mission Haut Brion    64  Bordeaux              France
Phelps Insignia          74  Cabernet Sauvignon    U.S.A.
Y'Quem                   58  Sauterne              France
Ridge Gyserville         73  Zinfandel             U.S.A.
```

Do I hear you murmur about a list by countries? Right away!

```
A>sort/+50 <b:wines <ENTER>

Lafite                    45  Bordeaux              France
La Mission Haut Brion     64  Bordeaux              France
Y'Quem                    58  Sauterne              France
Phelps Insignia           74  Cabernet Sauvignon U.S.A.
Ridge Gyserville          73  Zinfandel             U.S.A.
```

And when I think of all the years I spent alphabetizing by hand as I slowly muttered the alphabet under my breath. The beauty of SORT is that it is fun and functional.

Just as you can use a file as the input for the SORT command, you can also redirect the output to a file. For clarity's sake you would like to keep each sort in a separate file. This makes referencing your collection much quicker. To output the results of a sort to a file, just include the output reassignment character ">" in the command:

```
A>sort <b:wines >b:vintners <ENTER>
```

This command translates into DOS as *sort on column one the information in the "wines" file and put the output in a file called "vintners"*. When you perform a sort that redirects the output, you have assigned a new standard output device. Therefore, it follows that you will no longer see the sort on your regular standard output device, the screen. When SORT has transferred the results to a file, it returns you to the prompt:

```
A>
```

You can verify the new file by using DIR:

```
A>dir b:vintners <ENTER>

    Volume in drive B is WINE CELLAR
    Directory of B:\

VINTNERS          290     12-17-84    2:15P
        1 File(s)     360448 bytes free
```

Remember, the next time you want to add information to this "vintners" file you would need to use >> so that the output of the new SORT are appended to the contents of the "vintners" file:

```
A>sort <b:wines >>b:vintners <ENTER>
```

Using redirection, you can also create individual files to hold your other sorts:

```
A>sort/+23 <b:wines >b:years <ENTER>

A>sort/+28 <b:wines >b:type <ENTER>

A>sort/+52 <b:wines >b:country <ENTER>
```

When you have done all this your directory will look like this:

```
A>dir B:<ENTER>

    Volume in drive B is WINE CELLAR
    Directory of B:\

WINES          290     12-17-84    2:07P
VINTNERS       580     12-17-84    2:16P
YEARS          290     12-17-84    2:16P
```

```
TYPE              290    12-17-84    2:16P
COUNTRY           290    12-17-84    2:17P
        5 File(s)     357376 bytes free
```

The possibilities of SORT are intriguing. Not only does it rearrange your data very quickly, but, in conjunction with input and output redirection, it becomes a really powerful tool as well.

But you don't have to limit the use of SORT to files. Like all filters, it is really the most useful in piping. You can use the output of a command as input into the SORT filter.

You create a piping sequence by separating the various commands, filters, and files with the vertical bar character (|). For example:

```
dir | sort >b:alphadir
```

When using piping you leave a space before and after each vertical bar. The above command goes to the current directory, sorts the directory on the first column (since no options are included in the SORT command), and then puts the sorted directory into a file called "alphadir" on the diskette in drive B.

Let's try this using your system diskette:

```
A>dir | sort >b:alphadir <ENTER>
```

The directory won't be listed on the screen, but you will hear the drive working and the indicator light will be on. This is PIPE creating the temporary file that holds the output of DIR and the output of SORT. When the sorted directory is completed, it will be redirected to the file "alpahdir". If you want to see the sorted display, enter the command without output redirection:

```
A>dir | sort <ENTER>
```

In a few minutes the sorted listing will appear on the screen:

```
        25 File(s)       29696 bytes free

    Directory of A:\
    Volume in drive A has no label
%PIPE1    $$$         0  12-17-84   2:36P
%PIPE2    $$$         0  12-17-84   2:36P
ANSI      SYS      1664   3-08-83  12:00P
ASSIGN    COM       896   3-08-83  12:00P
BACKUP    COM      3687   3-08-83  12:00P
BASIC     COM     16256   3-08-83  12:00P
BASICA    COM     25984   3-08-83  12:00P
CHKDSK    COM      6400   3-08-83  12:00P
COMMAND   COM     17664   3-08-83  12:00P
COMP      COM      2523   3-08-83  12:00P
DISKCOMP  COM      2074   3-08-83  12:00P
DISKCOPY  COM      2444   3-08-83  12:00P
EDLIN     COM      4608   3-08-83  12:00P
FDISK     COM      6177   3-08-83  12:00P
FIND      EXE      5888   3-08-83  12:00P
FORMAT    COM      6106   3-08-83  12:00P
GRAPHICS  COM       789   3-08-83  12:00P
MODE      COM      3139   3-08-83  12:00P
MORE      COM       384   3-08-83  12:00P
PRINT     COM      4608   3-08-83  12:00P
RECOVER   COM      2304   3-08-83  12:00P
RESTORE   COM      4003   3-08-83  12:00P
SORT      EXE      1280   3-08-83  12:00P
SYS       COM      1408   3-08-83  12:00P
TREE      COM      1513   3-08-83  12:00P
```

Notice the first two files in the listing. These are the temporary "piping" files created during the SORT procedure. It is important to remember that when you SORT a file it *does not change the contents of the file*. The file remains in the same order as it was prior to the sort. For instance, if you performed the above sort on your system diskette, the sorted listing would not appear the next time you entered DIR. Instead, you would get the normal directory listing. This is why it is valuable to redirect the output of a SORT to a file if you want to use the sorted information again.

FIND is a fast and easy way to locate specific items in a file. FIND works with *strings*. A string is simply a group of characters enclosed in quotation marks. Like the SORT filter, FIND can receive input from a file or command and send it to any designated standard output device such as the screen, another file or program, or the printer.

Okay, now let's put FIND to work. One note of caution about the use of

---

The FIND Filter

use: locates strings within a file

switches: /v   display lines not containing the string
                 /c   display a count of the lines containing the string
                 /n   display the line number of lines containing the string

examples: find "France" b:wines
                find/v "France" b:wines
                find/c "France" b:wines
                find/n "France" b:wines
                dir | find "EXE"

---

strings. Strings within a file will be found only when they *exactly match* the enclosed string in the command. This includes the use of upper- and lowercase letters and all punctuation marks.

Suppose we want to find out which of our recent purchases were from France. Enter this command:

```
A>find "France" b:wines <ENTER>
```

Notice that you enter the command first, followed by the string, which must be enclosed in quotation marks. The name of the file to search is entered last. Every line containing the string will appear on the screen:

```
-------------- b:wines
Lafite                    45  Bordeaux              France
La Mission Haut Brion  64  Bordeaux              France
Y'Quem                    58  Sauterne              France
```

Yes, there are our three French wines.

Suppose you want a list of French wines, but you want it in alphabetical order. Then simply combine FIND in a pipeline with SORT:

```
A>find "France" b:wines : sort <ENTER>

-------------- b: wines
La Mission Haut Brion 64 Bordeaux          France
Lafite                45 Bordeaux          France
Y'Quem                58 Sauterne          France
```

Or if you want to, you can put this sorted French list into its own file for later reference:

```
A>find "France" b:wines : sort >b:French <ENTER>
```

The last command would not produce any display, of course, because you reassigned the output to be sent to the file "French".

There may be times when you want to FIND lines in a file that *do not* contain a specified string. FIND allows you to do this with the /v option. You want to list your American purchases:

```
A>find/v "France" b:wines <ENTER>
```

FIND works for a few seconds and produces this display:

```
-------------- b:wines
Phelps Insignia       74 Cabernet Sauvignon U.S.A.
Ridge Gyserville      73 Zinfandel          U.S.A.
```

But now you are reaching new, even more esoteric requirements. You want all non-French wines and you want them in alphabetical order:

```
A>sort <b:wines : find/v "France" <ENTER>
```

Now don't let the length of this command confuse you. Just take it one step at a time. It tells DOS: *sort the items in the "wines" file (on the first column since no column is listed), and then find all lines that do not display the string "France"*. See, it's not really confusing at all.

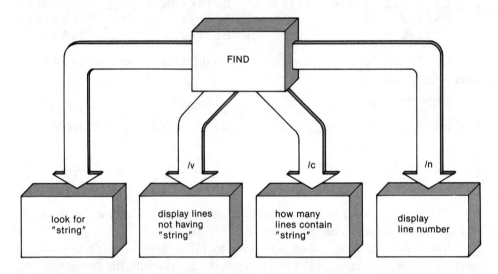

The FIND command.

Now let's suppose you are not particularly interested in the names of the French wines, you just want to know how many are in the file. Then you would use FIND with the /c switch. The /c switch returns a count of the lines containing the string:

```
A>find/c "France" b:wines <ENTER>
```

The response is the name of the file, followed by a number:

```
-------------- b:wines: 3
```

The final FIND option allows you to locate occurrences of the string very precisely. The /n switch displays the line number followed by the line itself, for every instance of the indicated string:

```
A>find/n "France" b:wines <ENTER>

-------------- b:wines
[1]Lafite                 45    Bordeaux      France
[4]La Mission Haut Brion  64    Bordeaux      France
[5]Y'Quem                 58    Sauterne      France
```

The line numbers indicate the position of the entries *in the original file*. For example, there are only three items in our display. Yet Y'Quem is assigned a line number of 5. This is because Y'Quem was the fifth entry in our original "b:wines" file.

Locating a string by line number can be very useful in large files. It is a fast and easy way to locate any type of string.

Just like the SORT filter, you don't need to limit the use of FIND to a display on the screen or a redirection to a file. You can also use it with commands. Try this combination on your system diskette:

```
A>dir | find "EXE" <ENTER>
```

Just ask and you shall receive:

```
SORT     EXE    1280    3-08-83    12:00P
FIND     EXE    5888    3-08-83    12:00P
```

FIND will take your request very literally. It will list not only the files with the extension EXE, but also any files that contain the string "EXE" within their filenames (e.g., AUTOEXEC.BAT).

Neither the SORT nor the FIND filters allow the use of global characters. It gets them hopelessly confused and the machine will just roll over and play dead if they are used in the filter command. One other unusual trick: in FIND, a quotation mark (") is interpreted as a search for an apostrophe ('). Well, everybody has little quirks.

At this point, you are probably realizing just how useful these filters are and shouting more, more. No sooner said, than done.

The MORE Filter

use: pauses in a display when the screen is filled

examples: more <b:wines
              dir ¦ more

Is a small voice in the back of your head telling you that stopping a scroll at the bottom of a filled screen is not totally unfamiliar? If so, give yourself a pat on the back. You saw this action when you used the /p (pause) switch with the DIR command (only in that case the message from MS-DOS was "Strike any key when ready").

MORE does the same thing in a filter form; it pauses at the bottom of the screen to make reading displays easier. This is how MORE would apply to our "wines" file:

```
A>more <b:wines <ENTER>
```

But stop. It's not really worth-while to enter this command because our "wines" file is less than one screen long in its entirety.

Let's use MORE in a *more* realistic situation. Switch back to your system diskette drive (unless you're there now) and try this command:

```
A>dir ¦ more <ENTER>
```

This directory contains 25 files, so it will take MS-DOS a few seconds to construct the temporary pipe files. But when it's finished, you should see the contents of your system diskette displayed until the screen is filled. The last line reads — More —. To get the remainder of the directory just press any key.

To FIND and SORT Still MORE

Now that you've learned about the SORT, FIND, and MORE filters and have examples on how they are used in piping and redirection, let's use them as building blocks to show how they can interact. You have come to the conclusion that it would really be easier to read your system diskette directory if the files were listed alphabetically and the display stopped scrolling automatically when the page was full. This is an eminently reasonable request:

```
A>dir | sort | more <ENTER>
```

And here is the answer to your needs:

```
          25 File(s) 29696 bytes free
     Directory of A:\
     Volume in drive A has no label
%PIPE1    $$$         0  12-17-84   2:45P
%PIPE2    $$$         0  12-17-84   2:45P
ANSI      SYS      1664   3-08-83  12:00P
ASSIGN    COM       896   3-08-83  12:00P
BACKUP    COM      3687   3-08-83  12:00P
BASIC     COM     16256   3-08-83  12:00P
BASICA    COM     25984   3-08-83  12:00P
CHKDSK    COM      6400   3-08-83  12:00P
COMMAND   COM     17664   3-08-83  12:00P
COMP      COM      2523   3-08-83  12:00P
DISKCOMP  COM      2074   3-08-83  12:00P
DISKCOPY  COM      2444   3-08-83  12:00P
EDLIN     COM      4608   3-08-83  12:00P
FDISK     COM      6177   3-08-83  12:00P
FIND      EXE      7000   3-08-83  12:00P
FORMAT    COM      6016   3-08-83  12:00P
```

```
GRAPHICS COM         789    3-08-83   12:00P
MODE     COM        3139    3-08-83   12:00P
-- MORE --
```

You press a key.

```
MORE     COM         384    3-08-83   12:00P
PRINT    COM        4608    3-08-83   12:00P
RECOVER  COM        2304    3-08-83   12:00P
RESTORE  COM        4003    3-08-83   12:00P
SORT     EXE        1280    3-08-83   12:00P
SYS      COM        1408    3-08-83   12:00P
TREE     COM        1513    3-08-83   12:00P
```

Another way to redesign the directory is to group all the same files together and then list them with the extensions in alphabetical order. To do this you need to know that the extension designation begins in column 10:

```
A>dir | sort/+10 | more <ENTER>
```

Wait a second, and here it is:

```
          25 File(s)        29696 bytes free
%PIPE1   $$$          0   12-17-84    2:52P
%PIPE2   $$$          0   12-17-84    2:52P
MORE     COM         384    3-08-83   12:00P
GRAPHICS COM         789    3-08-83   12:00P
ASSIGN   COM         896    3-08-83   12:00P
SYS      COM        1408    3-08-83   12:00P
TREE     COM        1513    3-08-83   12:00P
DISKCOMP COM        2074    3-08-83   12:00P
RECOVER  COM        2304    3-08-83   12:00P
DISKCOPY COM        2444    3-08-83   12:00P
COMP     COM        2523    3-08-83   12:00P
MODE     COM        3139    3-08-83   12:00P
BACKUP   COM        3687    3-08-83   12:00P
RESTORE  COM        4003    3-08-83   12:00P
EDLIN    COM        4608    3-08-83   12:00P
PRINT    COM        4608    3-08-83   12:00P
FORMAT   COM        6106    3-08-83   12:00P
FDISK    COM        6177    3-08-83   12:00P
```

```
CHKDSK     COM        6400     3-08-83    12:00P
BASIC      COM       16256     3-08-83    12:00P
-- More --
```
You press a key.
```
COMMAND    COM       17664     3-08-83    12:00P
BASICA     COM       25984     3-08-83    12:00P
SORT       EXE        1280     3-08-83    12:00P
FIND       EXE        5888     3-08-83    12:00P
ANSI       SYS        1664     3-08-83    12:00P
     Volume in drive A has no label
     Directory of A:\
```

You could attempt to SORT by date and/or time, but this is pretty useless. Why? Because SORT is very literal. If it is presented with these three dates:

9-05-80
5-02-83
7-16-82

it would SORT them like this:

5-02-83
7-16-82
9-05-80

In other words, SORT interprets 9-05-80 as *greater than* 5-02-83, so it puts it at the bottom of the list. As we demonstrated in our "wines" file when we sorted by year, you can successfully use numbers to SORT, but they must run consecutively. You could sort the system diskette by file size, for instance:

```
A>dir | sort/+17 | more <ENTER>
```

That concludes our discussion of these interesting and useful pipes and filters. Good plumbing!

In this chapter you learned about the various ways to use the redirection, piping, and sort features of MS-DOS. These are skills that will stand you in good stead as you use MS DOS more and more. The SORT, FIND, and MORE filters are very useful in reorganizing and using your data. The next chapter is for those of you who have a hard disk.

For Hard Disk Users

- Our Floppy Friends
- The New Kid on the Block
- Hard Disk Insurance
- Using Batch Files to Simplify Backup

11   For Hard Disk Users

This final chapter is for those of you who have a system with a built-in hard disk. It will give you some helpful pointers on using the commands associated with hard disks, BACKUP and RESTORE. For those of you who are not yet proud owners of a hard disk, but are interested in finding out some of its advantages and disadvantages, this chapter will start you on the path to knowledge.

Although you can buy a hard disk drive as an add-on peripheral to your computer, the installation and operation of these types of units will not be covered in this book.

Our Floppy Friends

No matter how many books you've read on "Proper Strategies of Computer System Purchase," or how many articles you've read on "Why Software Should Dictate Your Computer Type," once you get inside a computer store you may be overwhelmed. And the determining factor in your computer selection probably comes down to which machine is faster (you're buying it to save you time right?), or which machine is cheaper (everyone wants a good deal), or which one has the nicest monitor or the most built-in RAM or the convenience of a built-in printer. But one thing you may not pay too much attention to is how much storage capacity it has. And that's really a shame, because storage may be the most important factor in your computer use.

In fact, if you were not listening to your more experienced and well-intentioned friends, you may have bought a system with only one disk drive. If so, you probably have already discovered that with only one drive, and access to only one floppy at a time, the time spent in storing and retrieving data is a large part of your total time on the system. Most likely, however, you have a system with two floppy disk drives. And it serves you well.

But whether you have one drive or two, you have come to rely on the 5¼" floppy diskette as your storage media.

Floppy diskettes are certainly a vast improvement over the tape cartridges used for storage in the early "hobbyist" computers. Because of their small size, floppies are easy to use, convenient to store, and simple to mail. And since most computer system use a standard size of floppies, they can be used on many types of machines (subject to formatting restrictions, of course). This means that there is a huge market for floppies and, consequently, they are relatively inexpensive. Great! Terrific! Floppies are our friends.

But there are a few disadvantages to floppies. Since they are often inserted and removed from the drives, and sometimes left around carelessly, they can be easily damaged. And occasionally they do seem to wander off somewhere and get lost. But with careful handling, floppies perform for us. No, the two real disadvantages of floppies are that they have a rather limited capacity and they are slow.

Floppy diskettes hold about 200K to 400K bytes of information. That's pretty impressive for a 5¼″ circle of plastic, but unfortunately, it is nowhere near the amount of storage capacity that you need. So very early in your computer use you are quickly amazed at the number of floppies that you accumulate. As bigger and better programs are put on the market, using many diskettes, they add to your storage problems. And as you fill up diskettes, or dedicate certain diskettes to specific programs or data, the problem just accelerates.

For instance, the word-processing program I use is contained on one diskette. I usually have this diskette in drive A. The diskette in drive B holds the text I am working on. This setup works well until I want to use MS-DOS commands, or the EDLIN processor, or a BASIC program to create specific text or examples. When this situation arises, I have to first exit from the word-processing program, put a system diskette in drive A, put a new "examples" diskette in drive B, perform the operation, get a printout of the results, then reinsert the word-processing and text diskettes and enter the new information.

When I want to use a spelling checker, contained on two separate diskettes, the process becomes even more complicated. I have, on occasion, developed hand cramps from doing this "diskette shuffle."

The second real disadvantage of floppies is that they are slow. You may have noticed, now that you are a more experienced computer user, that most of your computer time is taken up with storing and retrieving data. In fact, preparing and checking diskettes, transferring data between the machine and the diskettes, reading in programs, and copying and erasing files is a real bottleneck in the smooth running of the computer system. Just compare how fast a computer can calculate with how long it takes to format a disk.

But let's not be too hard on our floppy friends, they are loyal and trusted compatriots and serve us well. It's just that there is an alternative.

The New Kid on the Block

Computer designers delight in the challenge of taking things originally created for big machines and adapting them for small machines. Remember this is how Microsoft's MS-DOS began, as an adaptation of an operating system running on a mainframe. This mainframe "environment" is where the concept of tree-structured directories was also born. It is no surprise that hard disks also have come to us via the big computer connection.

Hard disks have been in use in large computer systems for many years. But only with the adaptation of this technology to smaller units were they available as practical storage devices for personal computers. Many personal computer systems use a 10-megabyte hard disk. That means the disks can hold more than 10 million characters, or the equivalent of 30 floppy diskettes.

Floppy Diskettes Versus Hard Disks

Floppy Diskette	Hard Disk
Portable	Non-removable
Moderate access speed (250,000 bits/sec)	Fast access speed (5,000,000 bits/sec)
Capacity of 368,640 bytes	Capacity of 10,679,808 bytes
Need many for file storage	All files in one place
Quick backup	Slow backup
Inexpensive	Relatively expensive

Hard disks are so named because they are solid disks, magnetically coated like floppies, but sealed in a container that is never opened. Hard disks are very sensitive to smoke and other forms of damage. Compared to hard disks, floppies are indestructible. For this reason, many hard disks systems are sealed inside the computer unit where they can never get dirty, never get lost, and never need to reside in smoke-filled rooms. Even when hard disks are not actually located inside the computer, they are still sealed in their own protective case, which is permanently sealed.

In some ways it is inconvenient not to be able to get the disk out of the drive. In means that information you want to share must be copied to floppies. And it does make backing up data a bit more inconvenient. But because of its awesome storage capacity, the hard disk more than compensates for its disadvantages.

This enormous capacity means that you can have all your programs and data on tap, almost all the time. Accessing programs and files becomes much simpler. No more inserting and removing diskettes, no more lost information due to unlabeled diskettes or ones that can't be found. This is a real savings in time and frustration.

You don't have to be concerned about running out of room. Even if you did manage to fill up your hard disk to its maximum 10-megabyte capacity, you don't need to worry. You can transfer any information on a hard disk to a floppy, simply by using the COPY command. It's not as if you have to go out and buy a new hard disk when you reached 10 megabytes (hard disks are a bit expensive). Information can be transferred from the hard disk to floppies for storage. Of course, you can also put the information from the storage floppies back on the hard disk. This chapter discusses the commands that accomplish these transfers.

The second great thing about hard disks is that they are fast, roughly five times as fast as floppy diskettes. This means that while floppy diskettes have a moderate access speed of 250,000 bits/second, hard disks have an amazing access time of 5,000,000 bits/second. That's fast, folks! In fact, when you first begin using your hard disk, especially if you use a program you have often used on floppies, you'll be amazed at how fast your access time is.

Now before you start to think that hard disks are the best thing since sliced bread, let's take a small detour to look at the major disadvantage of hard disks. Surprisingly, the same thing that makes the disk so convenient, all your files in one place, is also a hazard. With all your information stored in one place, you must be doubly diligent about making backups. And backing up files from hard disk files is time-consuming.

It can take more than a half hour to copy all the files on a full hard disk to thirty floppies. You may ask *"What's the point in copying to floppies? Since there is so much room anyway, why bother to copy files?"* If you are going along with this philosophy, immediately turn to Chapter 4 and read "The Importance of Backups."

The reasons why you need backups for files stored on a hard disk are even more compelling than those for floppies. While the incidence of damage due to handling or storage is small, other factors are more overwhelming.

Remember, all your files are in one place and they are inside the machine.

This means that they are vulnerable to power failures or recurring power surges. One of these, and you could lose some or all of the data stored on your hard disk.

Importance Of Backups

All your files are in one place—all can be lost at once.

If there is a power surge or outage, the hard disk could become damaged.

While it is also unlikely that your hard disk will be damaged, the heads which read the information from the disk can cause damage to the disk's surface if dust or dirt gets into the system. Again, you are looking at potential catastrophe. So follow the old adage of "not putting all your eggs in one basket" and make a backup of hard disk files. Frequently.

Hard Disk Insurance

MS-DOS makes protecting your files easier with two commands, BACKUP and RESTORE. BACKUP is used to copy files from the hard disk to floppies RESTORE is used to put the files back on the hard disk.

Having amply demonstrated (we hope) the dire consequences of not making backups, we will begin with the BACKUP command.
Note: Before you can actually use your hard disk, it must be installed. This is a rather complicated process that requires some skill and is best left to your dealer the first time. Part of the installation procedure of your hard disk involves the question of partitioning. Partitioning, as you may expect, involves dividing up the hard disk into different areas. This is necessary because the hard disk has a very useful feature. It allows you to use more than one operating system on your system. But just as you can't mix apples and oranges, you can't mix operating systems. This means you can have UNIX or CP/M (two other operating systems) on your diskette. But the instructions for putting these systems on your diskette are specific to each operating system. The question of partitioning is really outside the scope of this book. Full instructions, however, can be found in your specific hard disk manual or in the part of your user's manual that deals with hard disks. For the purposes of our discussion, we will assume that you or your friendly computer store technician have installed your hard disk with the appropriate partitions. Our discussion will be limited to how to use the hard disk once it is up and running. It's easy to tell if your hard disk is ready. If you try to use it, and it is not operable, you will get this message:

```
Invalid drive specification
```

Be sure your hard disk is ready to go before you begin trying these commands.

The BACKUP Command

use: copies files from a hard disk to floppy diskettes

switches: /s   backup all files and subdirectories
            /m   backup all files modified since last backup
            /d   backup all files modified since a specific date
            /a   add the backup files to files already on floppy diskette

examples: backup fruits\cherries a:
            backup fruits\cherries a:/s
            backup C: A:/s
            backup C: A:/d:8-01-84
            backup fruits\cherries a:d:8-1-84/s
            backup fruits\cherries a:/a

The BACKUP program works a lot like the COPY command. That is, it copies the files from one device to the other, in this case, from the hard disk to a floppy. BACKUP has several useful switches that allow you to precisely define the files to be backed up.

You will notice in the examples above the use of the drive designator C:. This may confuse you. When you use a hard disk it is generally referred to as the C drive. Most hard disk systems also include one floppy disk drive. This floppy is referred to as drive A. We will use these designations when talking about the hard disk drive. For a further explanation of the use of drive designators with a hard disk see your operations manual.

Using BACKUP follows the same pattern as the COPY command. In response to the DOS prompt A> you first indicate the name of the file (with appropriate slashes if it is not part of the root directory) and then give the letter of the target diskette. You must use FORMAT to prepare the target diskette before issuing the command. To copy all of the files in FRUITS, *but not its subdirectories,* you enter:

```
A>backup fruits a: <ENTER>
```

You do not need to include the initial \ because FRUITS is part of the root directory. All the files in FRUITS are now copied to the floppy disk in drive A.

If you want to copy all the files in FRUITS *and include its subdirectories* you must use the /s switch.

```
A>backup fruits a:/s <ENTER>
```

This command copies the files in FRUITS ("weather" and "soil") and the contents of the subdirectory CHERRIES (the "yields" file), which is the only subdirectory in FRUITS.

You can also use BACKUP to copy only the files in a subdirectory of a subdirectory. To copy only the contents of FRUITS\CHERRIES you issue this command:

```
A>backup fruits\cherries a: <ENTER>
```

This copies all of the files in the CHERRIES subdirectory.

Remember, if there are subdirectories in the specified subdirectory and you want them included, you must indicate this by including the /s switch.

This may sound confusing at first. But if you have a copy of the TREE output for your hard disk, it will quickly tell you what files and subdirectories are included in each section of your overall directory.

You may also use the BACKUP command to copy the entire contents of the hard disk (like using *.* to copy all the files on a diskette). When you want to copy all the files and their associated subdirectories on a hard disk you enter this command:

```
A>backup c: a:/s <ENTER>
```

With this command you are instructing MS-DOS to copy everything on the hard disk (indicated by the c: drive designator) to the floppy in drive A. Of course, if you have lots of files, you will have to keep inserting new floppies until the entire copying procedure is completed. DOS will prompt you when a new diskette is needed.

To figure out how many formatted diskettes you need to have ready in order to copy the entire hard disk, you can use CHKDSK (yes, this works on a hard disk too!) to find the total number of bytes that you have used. You must then divide the number of bytes by 360,000 (the number of bytes that a floppy can hold) to find out how many floppies are needed. As mentioned earlier, backing up an entire hard disk can be very time-consuming. If you make periodic backups, it is only necessary to backup files you have created since the last backup. This is where the /m and /d switches come in handy.

The /m option lets you backup *only those files that you have modified* since the last BACKUP session. This can save you lots of time. Luckily for non-methodical users, you don't have to remember the last time you used a file (although you could get this information from the DIR command, but that could take a long time). No, built right into the BACKUP program is an internal "marker" that tells DOS if you have modified a file since your last BACKUP.

This command copies only those file in the \CHERRIES directory and its subdirectories that have been changed since the last BACKUP:

```
A>backup \cherries a:/s/m <ENTER>
```

Another way to backup new and modified files is to use the /d switch. This copies only files that were modified *after a certain date*. For example, you last backed up your files on August 1, 1984. It is now August 15, l984. You want to backup any files in the FRUITS directory that were created or modified since that date:

```
A>backup fruits a:/d:08-01-84 <ENTER>
```

If you wanted to backup files created after a specific date and any files that have been modified in any way (not necessarily related to any particular time), you would add the /s switch:

```
A>fruits a:/d:08-01-84/s <ENTER>
```

Of course, you can use these switches to copy all modified files on the entire hard disk by using the C: drive designator. But in practice it is probably a better idea to copy modified files in smaller increments, such as subdirectories, so you can assign certain subdirectories to specific floppies. If you just backup all your files in one huge move, it may be difficult to find specific files when you want to use the backup for some operation.

The /a switch tells MS-DOS to *add the backup files to any files already on the diskette* in the designated drive.

```
A>backup fruits\cherries a:/a <ENTER>
```

If you issue this command, all the files in FRUITS\CHERRIES will be added to the files on the diskette in drive A. Of course, you only need to include this switch if you want to save the files on the diskette.

If you do not specify this /a switch in the command, MS-DOS will prompt you to insert a formatted diskette. When you do not include /a in the command, all the files on the diskette in the designated drive are erased before any new files are written.

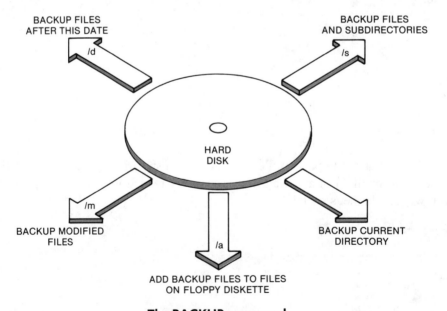

The BACKUP command.

BACKUP conveniently displays the name of the files it is copying. You can get a printout of the files you are backing up by using the control key combination ^P. This is a handy way to document the backup session and, if you write the number of the floppy which contains the files on the printout, it can provide a quick reference as to the location of your backup files.

Using Batch Files to Simplify Backup

Batch files, which were discussed in Chapter 8, can make the backup procedure easier for you. You will remember that batch files contain MS-DOS commands, and these include the commands used with the hard disk. One of the features of BACKUP is that it sets up an exit code value (a numerical marker which is MS-DOS's version of tying a string to its finger) when it is finished copying. This code ranges from 0 to 4:

0   indicates that everything was completed normally

1   indicates that DOS found no files to backup

2   for some reason this value is not used; they must be saving it to do something really esoteric!

3   indicates that the user terminated the backup procedure

4   indicates that the backup was terminated by an error

Glance back to the IF command that was discussed in the batch files section. You will see that IF can be used with ERRORLEVEL to cause a certain action to occur. By using IF in a batch file, you can automate the backup procedure and reduce the chance of making errors when performing backups. Using IF with BACKUP in a batch file is a good example of how useful and rewarding batch files can be. Here is how using ERRORLEVEL might clarify the operations going on in a batch file:

```
copy con: backall.bat
backup c: a/s
if errorlevel 0 echo backall completed
if errorlevel 1 echo backall failure
if errorlevel 3 echo you've terminated backall
if errorlevel 4 echo an error has terminated
backall
```

This discussion on backing up your hard disk has accomplished two things—it has impressed upon you the importance of backing up your hard disk files frequently and it has demonstrated the ins and outs of the BACKUP command.

Sometimes, when you first read about a command that is unfamiliar to you and has several switches, it may seem like just too much work. But BACKUP is really nothing more than COPY with a few added flourishes.

The entire rationale behind backing up files is, of course, to prepare for the worst, the loss of a file. After you have all your files safely stored away, the next question is *"How do I get them back on the hard disk from the floppies?"* The answer is the RESTORE command.

The RESTORE Command

use: copies one or more files from floppy diskettes to a hard disk

switches: /s include all subdirectories in the restoration
            /p check to see if the files being restored have been modified
                since they were last backed up

examples: restore a: c:fruits\cherries
            restore a: c:fruits/s

When you "restore" something you return it to its original condition, such as restoring furniture (or attempting to restore hair). But "restore" might also mean "store again." Both of these meanings tell you what this command does, it copies back your files from the diskette to the hard disk in the same form as they were when you last backed them up.

You can only use RESTORE with files that have been copied with the BACKUP command. Files that were copied using COPY won't work with this command. You provide the same information in the RESTORE command as you do in BACKUP: the source diskette, the target disk, and the name of the files to be copied. To restore all of the files in the FRUITS directory, you enter this command:

```
A>restore a: c:fruits <ENTER>
```

Once again, if you want to copy all the files and any subdirectories in the directory, you must include the /s switch:

```
A>restore a: c:fruits/s <ENTER>
```

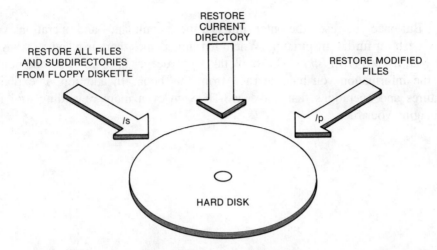

RESTORE ALL FILES
AND SUBDIRECTORIES
FROM FLOPPY DISKETTE

RESTORE
CURRENT
DIRECTORY

RESTORE MODIFIED
FILES

/s

/p

HARD DISK

The RESTORE command.

RESTORE also has another switch, /p. You include /p when you want to see if the files you are restoring have changed since they were last backed up. This prevents you from restoring a copy of the files that does not include recent modifications. (Of course, if you have not made a backup since modifying the file, you are out of luck. This is another good reason to make frequent backups.) Including /p verifies the files to be sure they are the latest version:

```
A>restore a: c:fruits\cherries/p <ENTER>
```

RESTORE can also be used with the IF command and the ERRORLEVEL option when the command is to be included in a batch file.

And really that's all there is to using your hard disk. BACKUP and RE-STORE are the only two commands in MS-DOS that are reserved for hard disk use. You can use all the other MS-DOS commands with your hard disk.

Because your computer system has a hard disk, you are one step ahead on the road to easier and faster computing. Good luck and enjoy!

This chapter presented some of the advantages and disadvantages of hard disks (the former outweigh the latter). You learned how to use the BACKUP and RESTORE commands to transfer files from hard disks to floppies and visa versa.

This concludes your journey of discovery through the MS-DOS operating system. You are now prepared to be the captain of your own ship as you chart new galaxies in MS-DOS space. This book presents all you need for a safe and rewarding journey.

But once you reach the outer limits of these commands and operations you may wish for further inspiration. When that time comes there is a source waiting for you, the *MS-DOS Bible*. This book takes you deeper into MS-DOS and builds on the information you have learned from this book. In addition, it explains features and operations that make MS-DOS an even more rewarding tool for managing your files.

Appendix

Error Messages

- Device Error Messages
- Additional Error Messages

Appendix   Error Messages

As in all things, you learn how to use MS-DOS by *doing*. And, since you are human, becoming acquainted with MS-DOS is a process in which you learn by trial and error. No matter how conscientious or diligent you are, you will make mistakes. Making mistakes and, then, correcting your mistakes is one of the most effective means of learning.

The designers of MS-DOS are no different than you. They make mistakes sometimes. To make things easier, they have documented many of the most common errors. That is why MS-DOS has *error messages*—to help you correct your mistakes.

There are many types of error messages. Those most frequently encountered are covered in this appendix. There are some messages that are not included. See your user's manual for a complete list of the messages to be found on your computer system.

This appendix divides error messages into two categories. The first covers error messages that refer to *devices*. The second lists messages that may or may not apply to a device, but which refer to MS-DOS commands or MS-DOS itself. The messages are listed in alphabetical order.

Device Error Messages

Device error messages are displayed if MS-DOS finds an error when it tries to use a device attached to the computer. These messages have a common format. It's easy to understand the message when you understand the format.

This format has two variations. The first is displayed when MS-DOS has a problem "reading" (trying to get information *from*) a device:

```
type error reading device
Abort, Retry, Ignore?
```

The second variation is displayed when MS-DOS has a problem "writing" (trying to put information *on*) a device:

```
type error writing device
Abort, Retry, Ignore?
```

Type defines the nature of this specific error and will vary with each instance. *Device* refers to the piece of hardware involved in the error, such as a disk drive or a printer.

The second line of our format offers you three options to recover from the error: abort, retry, ignore. MS-DOS is waiting for you to enter one of these options from the keyboard.

Before responding, check the obvious causes for the error. For instance, if the error concerns a disk drive, you may have left the door open or failed to insert the correct diskette. If the error indicates trouble with the printer, you may need to turn on the power or insert paper.

When you have checked all obvious causes, enter one of the three options:

R (Retry)   causes MS-DOS to try to perform the command or message again. This sometimes works even if you have not adjusted anything because the error might be minor and may not recur on the next try.

A (Abort)   causes MS-DOS to stop the operation in progress. You should enter this response if **R** fails to correct the error.

I (Ignore)   causes MS-DOS to retry the operation but ignore any errors it may encounter. It is not recommended that you use this response because it can result in losing data being read or written.

The following messages are those that might appear in the *type* section of the error message.

Bad call format   A driver is a part of the operating system that controls a specific input/output device, for instance, a modem or printer. Each driver has specific codes in MS-DOS. One such identifier is a "length request header." This message means an incorrect length request header was sent to the driver for the specified drive. Consult your dealer.

Bad command   The command issued to a *device* is invalid.

Bad unit   An incorrect "sub-unit number" (driver code) was sent to the driver for the specified drive. Consult your dealer. *See also* Bad call format.

Data   An error was detected while reading or writing data. Use CHKDSK to see if your diskette has a defective area.

Disk   After three tries, a disk read or write error is still occurring. You may have inserted the wrong type of diskette (single-sided diskette in a double-sided drive) or your diskette may be inserted wrong. If neither is true, you may have a bad diskette.

If you receive the above message, try the standard corrective procedures before removing the diskette. You may be able to salvage the data on the diskette.

File allocation table bad, drive *d*   This message always refers to a specific disk drive. It tells you that the file allocation table (FAT) on the indicated drive is faulty. If you receive this error frequently, the diskette is probably defective.

No paper   This is an easy one to solve. There isn't any paper in your printer or the printer is not turned on. Correct the problem and press R.

Non-DOS disk   There is invalid data on the allocation table of the specified diskette in the indicated device. The diskette needs to be reformatted or the entire diskette may be wiped out.

Not ready   The device is not ready to read or write data. This may mean that the power is not turned on, the drive door is not closed, or there is no diskette in the indicated drive.

Read fault   For some reason the device cannot receive or transmit data. The power may not be on, the drive may not contain a diskette, or the device is not properly configured for MS-DOS use.

Sector not found   The sector holding the data you want cannot be located. The diskette may be defective or you may be using a single-sided diskette in a double-sided drive.

Seek error   MS-DOS cannot locate the proper track on the diskette in the indicated drive.

Write fault   For some reason the device cannot receive or transmit data. The power may not be on, the drive may not contain a diskette, or the device is not properly configured for MS-DOS use.

Write protect   You have instructed MS-DOS to write to a diskette that is write-protected (either temporarily by you or permanently by the manufacturer). Either insert a new diskette or remove the write-protect tab from this diskette (be sure you want to write to it first). If there is no write-protect notch, you are out of luck.

Additional Error Messages

Again, this is not a complete listing of all other error messages which may be received from MS-DOS. Check your system manual if you cannot locate the message either in the "Device Error Messages" or in this section.

Some error messages are associated with a specific command. When this is the case, the command has been written following the error message.

All specified file(s) are contiguous   *CHKDSK*. All the files that you requested to write are on the diskette sequentially.

Allocation error, size adjusted   *CHKDSK*. There was an invalid sector number in the file allocation table. The indicated filename was truncated at the end of the previous good sector.

Attempted write-protect violation   *FORMAT*. You attempted to FORMAT a write-protected diskette. Remove the diskette and insert a new one.

Bad command or filename   You entered the command or filename incorrectly. Check the spelling and punctuation and make sure the command or file you specified is on the diskette in the indicated drive. You may be calling an external command from a diskette that does not contain the command.

Cannot edit .BAK file - rename file   To protect your data, you cannot access a backup file that has a .BAK extension. Rename the file using REN, or copy the file, giving it a new name.

Cannot load COMMAND, system halted   While attempting to load the command processor, MS-DOS found that the area in which it keeps track of available memory is destroyed. Try booting MS-DOS again.

Contains *xxx* non-contiguous blocks   *CHKDSK*. The indicated file has been written in sections on different areas on the diskette (rather than in sequential blocks). Since fragmented files take longer to read, it is probably best to copy the file sequentially.

Disk boot failure   While trying to load MS-DOS, an error was encountered. If this continues, use a backup MS-DOS diskette.

Disk error writing FAT *x*   *CHKDSK*. There was a disk error while CHKDSK was trying to update the FAT on the indicated drive. *X* will be a 1 or a 2, depending on which of the allocation tables could not be written. If both allocation tables are indicated, the diskette is unusable.

Duplicate filename or file not found   *RENAME*. The name you indicated in a RENAME command already exists on the diskette or the file to be renamed is not on the diskette in the specified drive.

Entry error   *EDLIN*. Your last command contains a syntax error.

Error loading operating system   An error was encountered while trying to load the operating system from the fixed (hard) disk. If the problem persists, load MS-DOS from a diskette and use SYS to copy MS-DOS to the fixed disk.

File cannot be copied onto itself   You tried to give an already existing filename to a new file in the same directory.

File not found   The file named in a command parameter could not be found, or the command could not be found on the specified drive.

Incorrect DOS version   You attempted to run an MS-DOS command that requires a different version of MS-DOS. This should occur only when you are using MS-DOS Version 1.0 or 1.1 and attempt to use a command found only in MS-DOS Version 2.0 or higher.

Insufficient disk space   There is not enough free space on the diskette to hold the file you are writing. If you think there should be enough space, use CHKDSK to get a diskette status report.

Intermediate file error during pipe   This message may mean that the intermediate files created during a piping procedure cannot be accommodated on the diskette because the default drive's root directory is full. Your diskette may also be too full to hold the data being piped or the piping files cannot be located on the diskette.

Invalid COMMAND.COM in drive *d*   While trying to reload the command processor, MS-DOS found that the copy of COMMAND.COM on the diskette is a different version. Insert a diskette containing the correct version of MS-DOS.

Invalid directory   One of the directories in the specified pathname does not exist.

Invalid number of parameters   The specified number of parameters does not agree with the number required by the command.

Label not found   *GOTO #*. You have named a label in a GOTO command that does not exist in the batch file. Use EDLIN to review GOTO and make sure all GOTO statements contain valid labels.

No room for system on diskette   *SYS*. The specified diskette does not contain the required reserved space for the system. (Is the system already on the diskette?) You can solve this problem by using FORMAT/s to format a new diskette and then copying your files to this diskette.

Syntax error The command was entered incorrectly. Check the format.

Terminate batch job (Y/N)? You have pressed <Ctrl> <Break> or <Ctrl> C during the processing of a batch file. Press Y to end processing. Press N to stop the command that was executing when you pressed <Ctrl> <Break> or <Ctrl> C; processing will continue with the next command.

Index

MS-DOS Reference Card

<table>
<tr><td colspan="2">

Command Notation

</td></tr>
<tr><td>boldface</td><td>Items in boldface must be entered. You may use either upper- or lowercase.</td></tr>
<tr><td>italics</td><td>Items in italics are variables. d is the drive, filespec is the name of your file, pathname is the directory path, and line is the line number.</td></tr>
<tr><td>[ ]</td><td>Items in square brackets [ ] are optional. Do not enter the brackets, only the optional information.</td></tr>
<tr><td>|</td><td>Items separated by a vertical bar | are either/or entries. ON|OFF means either ON or OFF.</td></tr>
<tr><td>. . .</td><td>An ellipsis . . . following items means you may repeat the items as often as needed.</td></tr>
<tr><td>punctuation</td><td>Include all punctuation marks as shown, including commas, colons, semicolons, question marks, slashes, and quotes. Also include any parentheses and plus signs. Do not include square brackets, vertical bars, and ellipses.</td></tr>
</table>

MS-DOS Commands

BACKUP   back up hard disk files
BACKUP [*d:*][*pathname*][*filespec*]***d:***[/S][/M][/A]
    [/D:*mm-dd-yy*]

CHKDSK   check disk, give status
CHKDSK [*d:*][*filespec*][/F][/V]

CLS   clear display screen
CLS

COPY   copy files
COPY [*d:*][*pathname*]***source filespec***[*d:*][*pathname*]
    [*target filespec*]
or
COPY [*d:*][*pathname*]***source filespec***[+ [*d:*][*pathname*]
    source filespec...][*d:*][*pathname*][*target filespec*]

DIR   list directory
DIR [*d:*][*pathname*][*filespec*][/P][/W]

DISKCOPY   copy a diskette
DISKCOPY [*d:*] [*d:*]

ERASE   erase a file
ERASE [*d:*][*pathname*][*filespec*]
or
DEL
DEL [*d:*][*pathname*][*filespec*]

FORMAT   format a disk
FORMAT [*d:*][/S][/V]

MODE   set I/O devices
MODE LPT#:[*n*][,[*m*][,P]]
where:
# = 1, 2, or 3
n = 80 or 132 (characters/line)
m = 6 or 8 (lines/inch)

Wildcards

*   (asterisk) use for up to eight positions in a filename and up to three positions in an extension

?   (question mark) use for any single character in filename or extension

Control Keys

\<BACKSPACE\>   move to left along line and erase characters
or \<←\>

\<Caps Lock\>   enter all alphabetic keys in uppercase

\<ENTER\>   indicate end of an entry
or \<⏎ \>

\<Esc\>   cancel current line

\<Num Lock\>   switch between numeric and cursor control modes
\<Ctrl\> \<Num Lock\> stop the screen from scrolling

\<PrtSc\>   route information to printer
\<SHIFT\> \<PrtSc\> print entire screen
\<Ctrl\> \<PrtSc\> echo each line to printer

Control Key Combinations

\<Ctrl\> \<Alt\> \<Del\>   reboot system

\<Ctrl\> C   cancel current line or current program

\<Ctrl\> H   move cursor to the left and erase characters

\<Ctrl\> N   turn off echoing function

\<Ctrl\> P   echo display to the printer

\<Ctrl\> S   stop scrolling (press any key to resume)

\<Ctrl\> Z   end of file marker

DOS Editing Keys

\<F1\>   copy one character—copy the next character in template

\<F2\>   copy up to—copy up to specified character

\<F3\>   copy all—copy entire template

\<F4\>   skip up to—skip up to specified character

\<F5\>   create new template—make most recent line the template; does not execute command

\<Del\>   skip over one character—skip over next character in template

\<Ins\>   insert characters—insert new characters into existing template

\<Esc\>   cancel current line—template not affected

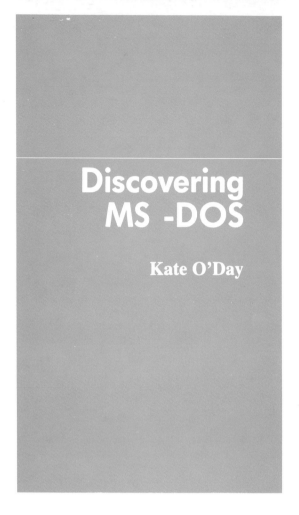

Discovering
MS -DOS

Kate O'Day

Reference Card

Howard W. Sams & Co.
A Division of Macmillan, Inc.
4300 West 62nd Street
Indianapolis, IN 46268 USA

MS-DOS is a trademark of Microsoft Corporation

HOWARD W. SAMS & COMPANY

The Waite Group

Advanced C Primer ++
Stephen Prata, The Waite Group

Programmers, students, managers, and hackers will learn to master the C programming language. Anyone who knows the basics of C will learn practical C tips never before published.
ISBN: 0-672-22486-0, $23.95

C Primer Plus, Revised Edition
Waite, Prata, and Martin, The Waite Group

The perfect tutorial for beginning C programmers and students, this book includes key additions about the C language and object-oriented programming using C++.
ISBN: 0-672-22582-4, $23.95

Microsoft® C on the IBM® PC
Robert Lafore, The Waite Group

A tutorial for the beginning programmer with enough information to write useful and marketable programs for the IBM PC family, featuring hands-on interaction with the C compiler and the PC.
ISBN: 0-672-22515-8, $24.95

Inside XENIX®
Christopher L. Morgan, The Waite Group

Through easily-read-and-understood XENIX references and tutorials, this comprehensive text examines in detail its unique internal structure including its shells and utilities.
ISBN: 0-672-22445-3, $21.95

Advanced UNIX® — A Programmer's Guide
Stephen Prata, The Waite Group

An advanced guidebook beyond the basics of UNIX and with details of the system's key components and various programming mechanisms. It shows how to use simple and complex commands, including the Bourne Shell, shell scripts, loops, and system calls.
ISBN: 0-672-22403-8, $21.95

Tricks of the UNIX® Masters
Russell G. Sage, The Waite Group

This book contains the shortcuts, tips, tricks, and secrets programmers want, using a "cookbook" approach ranging from I/O functions and file operations to porting UNIX to a different computer.
ISBN: 0-672-22449-6, $22.95

UNIX® Primer Plus
Waite, Martin, and Prata, The Waite Group

Learn about the amazing UNIX operating system as this book presents UNIX in a clear, simple, and easy-to-understand style. It is fully illustrated and includes two summary cards for quick reference.
ISBN: 0-672-22028-8, $19.95

UNIX® System V Primer, Revised Edition
Waite, Martin, and Prata, The Waite Group

This edition provides a comprehensive overview and introduction to the UNIX System V operating system for the beginner, including a new chapter on the extended electronic mail program and the use of the new shell layer manager.
ISBN: 0-672-22570-0, $22.95

UNIX® Communications
Bryan Costales, The Waite Group

This book will clarify the complexities of the UNIX communication facilities. It gathers the knowledge and techniques needed to use, administer, and program UNIX-to-UNIX communication and UNIX mail.
ISBN: 0-672-22511-5, $26.95

UNIX® System V Bible
Prata and Martin, The Waite Group

This is a comprehensive reference for programmers working with the UNIX operating system documentation, covering intermediate to advanced level programming for professionals who have prior experience programming in C or using UNIX.
ISBN: 0-672-22562-X, $24.95

UNIX® Papers
Edited by The Waite Group

Collection of learning tutorials, issue papers, and case histories that provide insightful information on the UNIX operating system and UNIX business market, revealing the more hidden and obscure truths about UNIX.
ISBN: 0-672-22578-6, $26.95

Discovering MS-DOS®
Kate O'Day, The Waite Group

This comprehensive study of MS-DOS commands begins with information about operating systems then shows how to produce letters and documents; create, name, and manipulate files; use the keyboard and function keys to perform jobs faster; and direct, sort, and find data quickly.
ISBN: 0-672-22407-0, $15.95

MS-DOS® Bible
Steven Simrin, The Waite Group

This book helps intermediate users explore this operating system's capabilities from system start-up to creating, editing, and managing files, handling data, and customizing the keyboard. It includes detailed coverage of the tree-structured directories and DOS filters.
ISBN: 0-672-22408-9, $18.95

MS-DOS® Developer's Guide
Angermeyer and Jaeger, The Waite Group

This is a guide for programmers with a working knowledge of 8088 ALC, who want to learn tricks for getting their software running in the MS-DOS environment. Included are assembly coding tips, explanations, MS-DOS versions, and higher-level language debuggers and aids.
ISBN: 0-672-22409-7, $24.95

Understanding MS-DOS®
O'Day and Angermeyer, The Waite Group

This introduction to the use and operation of the MS-DOS operating system includes fundamentals and advanced features of the operating system.
ISBN: 0-672-27067-6, $16.95

HOWARD W. SAMS & COMPANY

The Waite Group

Product Number	Quantity	Price	Total

Subtotal	
All states please add sales tax	
Standard shipping & handling	$2.50
Total	

Name_____

Title/Company_____

Address_____

City_____

State/Zip_____

Signature (required)_____

☐ Check ☐ Money Order ☐ MC ☐ VISA ☐ AE

Account #_____ Exp. Date·____

To order by phone call 800-428-SAMS.

Offer good in U.S.A. only. Prices and availability subject to change without notice. Full payment must accompany your order.

WC 344